Controller's Guide
to Costing

Controller's Guide to Costing

by
Steven M. Bragg

WILEY

John Wiley & Sons, Inc.

These chapters first appeared in *Cost Accounting: A Comprehensive Guide* by Steven M. Bragg.
Copyright 2001, Chapters 9–18.

Library of Congress Cataloging-in-Publication Data

Bragg, Steven M.
   Controller's guide to costing / Steven M. Bragg
     p. cm.
   Includes index.
   ISBN 0-471-71394-5 (cloth)
   1. Cost accounting. I. Title.

  HF5686.C8B6728 2005
  657′.42—dc22   2004058383

Printed in the United States of America

10 9 8 7 6 5 4 3 2 1

I first talked to Wiley editor Sheck Cho during a conference call in 1994. Over the subsequent ten years, we have collaborated on a multitude of accounting management books. Sheck, thanks for trusting a new author so long ago and for sticking with me for all the intervening years.

Contents

Preface

The modern coporate controller has many duties, including budgeting, tax planning, dealing with auditors, creating financial statements, and monitoring control systems. All are important, but at the core of the controller's job is a thorough understanding of a company's cost structure. Without this knowledge base, the controller is much less capable of predicting expenses, recommending operational changes, or evaluating the performance of business units.

This book supplies the necessary knowledge by covering every major costing methodology: the traditional job and process costing concepts, as well as direct costing, standard costing, and several inventory layering techniques—all techniques with some application in most organizations. In addition, other chapters address more specialized costing methodologies, such as throughput accounting for bottleneck analysis, target costing for new product decision making, and activity-based costing for more precise cost application. These costing methodologies sometimes vary considerably from each other in their purposes, so a costing systems summary is also included that identifies which technique to use for a different objective; specific recommendations are made regarding such key management decisions as outsourcing, cost reduction analysis, scrap costing, and capacity utilization.

Most chapters describe the advantages and disadvantages of a specific costing methodology, key terminology, and the flow of data through the system, including specific journal entries where applicable. Also, as is becoming more important through the requirements of the Sarbanes-Oxley Act, several chapters describe control point issues associated with a costing system. Additional topics are addressed where they are relevant to a specific costing methodology, such as the impact of direct costing on reported financial results, the formulation of standard costs, the use of throughput accounting for capital budgeting decisions, joint cost allocation methods, and using a bill of activities within an activity-based costing system. Where applicable, case studies assist in giving a greater understanding of key costing concepts.

Using this book, which condenses such a broad range of costing information into one book, the controller can gain a solid understanding of every major costing methodology without having to purchase and peruse an entire library of accounting books, each one treating a single costing topic. Further, the controller will find that this book provides a wide array of costing tools with which to analyze and resolve many key management issues.

STEVEN M. BRAGG
Centennial, Colorado
February 2005

About the Author

Steven Bragg, CPA, CMA, CIA, CPIM, has been the chief financial officer or controller of four companies, as well as a consulting manager at Ernst & Young and auditor at Deloitte & Touche. He received a master's degree in finance from Bentley College, an MBA from Babson College, and a bachelor's degree in Economics from the University of Maine. He has been the two-time president of the 10,000-member Colorado Mountain Club and is an avid alpine skier, mountain biker, and certified master diver. Mr. Bragg resides in Centennial, Colorado.

More Books by Steven M. Bragg

Accounting and Finance for Your Small Business (Wiley)
Accounting Best Practices (Wiley)
Accounting Reference Desktop (Wiley)
Advanced Accounting Systems
Billing and Collections Best Practices (Wiley)
Business Ratios and Formulas (Wiley)
Controller's Guide to Planning and Controlling Operations (Wiley)
Controllership (Wiley)
Cost Accounting (Wiley)
Design and Maintenance of Accounting Manuals (Wiley)
Essentials of Payroll (Wiley)
Financial Analysis (Wiley)
GAAP Implementation Guide (Wiley)
Inventory Best Practices (Wiley)
Inventory Accounting (Wiley)
Just-in-Time Accounting (Wiley)
Managing Explosive Corporate Growth (Wiley)
Outsourcing (Wiley)
Payroll Accounting (Wiley)
Planning and Controlling Operations (Wiley)
Run the Rockies (CMC Press)
Sales and Operations for Your Small Business (Wiley)
The Controller's Function (Wiley)
The New CFO Financial Leadership Manual (Wiley)

Controller's Guide to Costing

1

Job Costing

Job costing is the most common method for marshaling cost accounting information into a data structure containing usable information. Most cost accountants have experienced this system at some point in their careers, quite possibly at every facility where they have ever worked. In this chapter we consider the nature of job costing and why it is used so frequently. In addition, we present a graphical representation of how data flows through this system and then proceed to a discussion of the main control points to be aware of and how they can fail.

NATURE OF JOB COSTING

As the name implies, job costing is designed to accumulate the costs of small batches, or jobs, of products. This may mean that a single job is considered a single product created in volumes of one, or much larger batches produced for several weeks or months—it all depends on the production process.

In essence, job costing traces all material and direct labor costs directly to a batch and allocates overhead costs to batches as well. This is a simple rendition of the system. In reality it must first accumulate costs for any components or subassemblies stored in inventory and then shift these costs to specific jobs once the items are taken from stock and assigned to a job. It also requires direct labor employees to charge their time to specific jobs (which necessitates a good timekeeping system). In addition, overhead costs must be

1

stored in separate cost pools and then allocated to each job. These overhead costs can be allocated using a standard overhead rate, which is called *normal* costing, or they can be allocated with actual costs, which is (predictably) called *actual* costing. The result is a computer file on each job that itemizes all the direct material, direct labor, and overhead costs that have been assigned to it. In the next section we consider the advantages and disadvantages of this method and then go on to present a more in-depth review of the transactions that flow through the system.

ADVANTAGES AND DISADVANTAGES OF JOB COSTING

One of the primary advantages of job costing is that the management team has ready access to all the costs incurred for each job being completed. This allows the team to examine each cost incurred, finding out why it happened, and determine how it can be controlled better in the future, thereby contributing to better ongoing levels of profitability. For example, a proper job record contains any special reworking costs, which a manager can then use to trace back to the specific reason why the rework was needed. Similarly, overhead allocations based on machine usage reveal problems with excess use, which might be the result of lengthy machine setups or breakdowns as well as longer-than-expected machine cycle times.

Another reason for using job costing is that it yields ongoing results for each job. In today's world of fully computerized production tracking databases, one can use a job costing system to track costs as they are added to a job rather than waiting until the job has been completed. This gives a company several advantages. One is that the accounting staff can monitor job accounts to see if costs are being posted to the wrong accounts and correct them right away, rather than waiting until the job closes and having to frantically review records to see why the results are different from expectations. Another advantage is that a company can monitor the costs incurred for longer jobs and have enough time to make changes before they close, based on the costing information revealed by the job costing system. For example, a lengthy new-product development project might be over budget after just 25% of the work has been completed; if the management team is made aware of this costing problem early in the project, it will still have 75% of the project in which to make corrections and bring costs back down to budgeted levels. Yet a third advantage is that changes in the cost of a job can result in negotiations with cost-plus customers who are paying for all the costs incurred, so that they are fully aware of cost overruns well in advance and are prepared to pay the additional amounts. All these factors are the main advantages of using job costing in a computerized environment.

There are also several problems with job costing. One is that it focuses attention primarily on products rather than on departments or activities. This is not an issue if there are supplemental systems in place that record information about these other cost categories, but it leaves management with inadequate information if this is not the case. Another difficulty is that overhead is generally allocated based on rates that are changed only about once a year. Considerable fluctuation in overhead costs over the course of a year can result in both over- and underallocation of overhead costs to jobs during that period. Another problem is specific to the use of normal costing. As noted in the last section, this practice involves the use of a standard overhead rate rather than one that is based on actual costs and requires adjustment from time to time. If it is management's intention to charge individual jobs for the variance between standard and actual overhead rates, this may not be possible if some jobs have already been closed by the time the variance allocation takes place. This is not just a technical accounting issue, for some jobs are fully reimbursed by customers who pay on a cost-plus basis; if the overhead variance is a positive one, a company may not be able to charge its customers for the added costs if the related jobs have already been closed.

Another issue is that job costing has little relevance in some environments. For example, the software industry has high development costs but almost zero direct costs associated with the sale of its products. The use of a job costing system to record these costs makes little sense if the associated costs represent only a few percent of the total revenue gained from each one. The same problem arises in service industries, such as retailing, where there is no discernible product. These situations limit the most effective use of job costing to two areas—production and professional services. The first case, production, is an obvious use for the concept since there are high material costs that can be specifically identified with a job. The same is true of professional services, but here the main cost is direct labor rather than direct materials. In most other cases job costing does not provide management with a sufficient quantity of information to be useful.

The most important problem with job costing is that it requires a major amount of data entry and data accuracy in order to yield effective results. Data related to materials, labor, overhead, indirect labor, scrap, spoilage, and supplies must be entered into a system capable of accurately assigning these costs to the correct jobs every time. In reality such systems are rife with mistakes due to the sheer volume of data transactions, keying errors, misidentification of jobs, and the like. Problems can be resolved with a sufficient amount of error tracing by the accounting staff, but there may be so many that there are not enough staff members to keep up with them. Though these issues can to some degree be resolved through the use of computerized data entry systems, one may still have to determine whether the cost of maintaining such a system outweighs the benefits to be gained from it.

A final issue is that a large proportion of the costs assigned to a job, frequently more than 50%, comes from allocated overhead. When there is no fully proven method for accurately allocating overhead, such as through an activity-based costing system (Chapter 8), the results of the allocation yield meaningless information. This has been a particular problem for companies that persist in allocating overhead costs based on the direct labor used by each job, since a small amount of labor is generally being used to allocate a much larger amount of overhead, resulting in large shifts in overhead allocations based on small changes in labor costs. Some companies avoid this problem by ignoring overhead for job costing purposes or by reducing overhead cost pools to include only overhead directly traceable at the job level. In this way, many costs are not allocated to jobs at all, but those that are allocated are fully justifiable.

Clearly, one must weigh the pros and cons of using a job costing system to see if the benefits outweigh the costs. This system is a complex one that is prone to error, but it does yield good information about product-specific costs.

JOB COSTING DATA FLOW

In this section we consider the most common transactions encountered when using a job costing system. These transactions are noted graphically in Exhibits 1.1 through 1.4, each of which indicates the journal entries used. In these exhibits, journal entries are contained within rectangles showing the accounts that are debited and credited, as well as transaction descriptions (in bold) at the bottom of each rectangle.

Three types of transactions flow through a job costing system. The first is related to direct materials and is shown in Exhibit 1.1. As noted at the top of the exhibit, materials are purchased by a company and stored in inventory on receipt. When they are pulled from stock and issued to a job, a second transaction shifts the cost of these materials out of inventory and into work in process ("WIP Inventory"). There should be a subledger in the accounting system that stores these material costs by specific job and then summarizes this information into a single lump-sum entry in the general ledger (thereby keeping the general ledger from becoming too cluttered with entries). As the materials are used in the production process for each job, there may be abnormal amounts of scrap or spoilage; if so, the cost of these quantities is charged directly to the cost of goods sold. Alternatively, the cost of any expected, or normal, scrap and spoilage is charged to an overhead cost pool for later allocation back to jobs. These two transactions are noted on the left side of the exhibit. Once each job is finished, a transaction shifts its total cost from work in process to finished goods. Finally, when there is a sales transaction, the cost of the finished goods is shifted to the cost of goods sold and the sale is recorded in a separate journal entry. These transactions are noted at the bottom of Exhibit 1.1 and are the primary job costing transactions related to direct materials.

The second type of transaction that flows through a job costing system is for labor and is detailed in Exhibit 1.2. It begins with the incurrence of labor, for which there is a journal entry to wages expense and wages payable. The wages payable is eventually cleared with an offset to the cash account, but this issue falls outside the job costing system. The main problem is what happens to the wages expense. It comprises both direct and indirect labor. As noted on the right side

Exhibit 1.1 Job Costing Transactions for Direct Materials

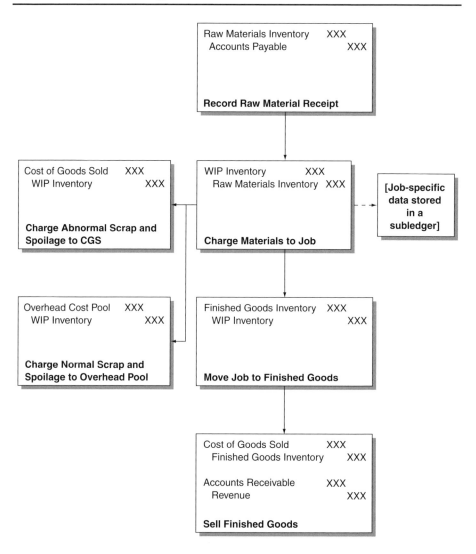

of the exhibit, direct labor costs are shifted from the wages expense account to the work-in-process account, where they are itemized by job in a subsidiary ledger. As was the case for direct materials, these individual job records are rolled up into a summary-level account in the general ledger. Indirect labor (i.e., any labor that cannot be directly ascribed to a specific job) is charged to an overhead cost pool

Exhibit 1.2 Job Costing Transactions for Labor

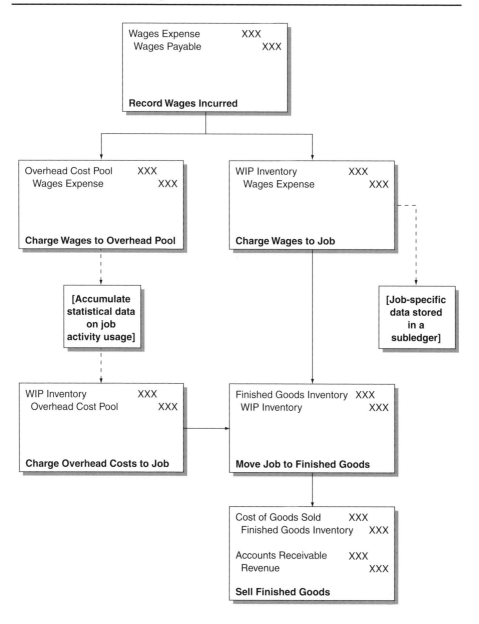

Exhibit 1.3 Job Costing Transactions for Actual Overhead Cost Allocations

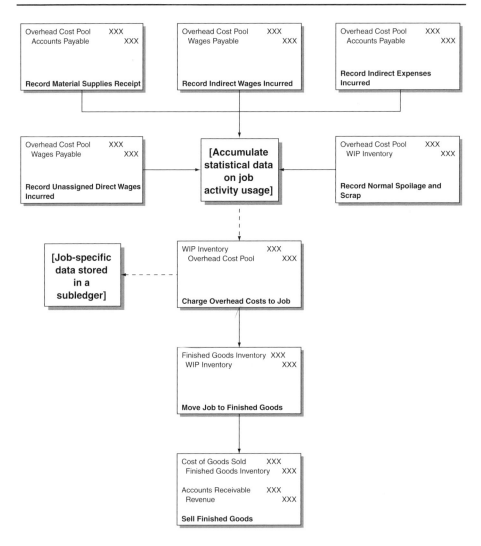

as noted on the left side of the exhibit. These costs are later allocated back to jobs, as noted in Exhibit 1.3. Finally, at the bottom of Exhibit 1.2, we see the same transactions that shift completed jobs from work in process to finished goods and then to the cost of goods sold. These are the primary job costing transactions related to labor.

Exhibit 1.4 Job Costing Transactions for Normal Overhead Cost Allocations

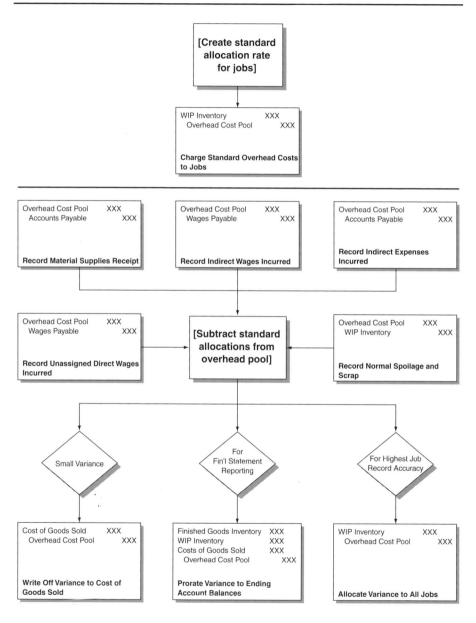

The third type of job costing transaction is related to overhead costs. As indicated in Exhibit 1.3, overhead costs are summarized into one or more cost pools and then allocated to all open jobs based on some activity measure. Exhibit 1.3 presents the flow of transactions based on the assumption that actual costing is being used for the overhead allocation process; the normal costing process flow is presented in the next exhibit.

The transaction flow begins with the accumulation of costs into an overhead cost pool. There are a number of sources of these costs. Material supplies (i.e., materials not directly traceable to a specific job) are charged to an overhead cost pool as soon as they are purchased, since they are not stored in the inventory account. Indirect wages, as just noted, are also charged to an overhead cost pool. In addition, there are a number of other expenses, such as utilities and insurance, that are charged directly to a cost pool as soon as bills are received from suppliers. Likewise, several variances from direct labor and direct materials are charged to overhead. One is for direct labor that has not been specifically charged to a job, and another is any normal spoilage or scrap from direct materials. All these journal entries are noted in the top half of Exhibit 1.3. These costs can be accumulated into different overhead cost pools if the activity measures used to allocate them to jobs are substantially different. For example, a cost pool that accumulates all material handling costs can allocate costs based on the number of material moves required for each job, whereas another cost pool for machine-related expenses charges out its costs based on the minutes of machine use by each job. The number and type of cost pools used are based on the activity measures employed and the utility of the resulting increases in the accuracy of allocations. See Chapter 8 for a lengthier description of this topic.

The next step in the cost allocation process is to determine an activity measure to use for allocating the costs in each pool to the various open jobs (again, see Chapter 8 for a discussion of allocation methods). Next, one must accumulate statistics on the amount of each activity used by each job and then allocate costs from the cost pools to the jobs based on the amounts of each activity used. This results in the journal entry in the middle of Exhibit 1.3, where we debit the work-in-process account and credit the overhead cost pool account. We then finish with the usual transactions that shift costs from work in process to finished goods on completion of each job, and from there to the cost of goods sold when each job is sold.

An alternative to allocating direct costs is to use the normal costing approach as outlined in Exhibit 1.4. With this method, we create a standard allocation rate per unit of activity rather than using the actual cost. This is done in order to facilitate the allocation of costs, which may otherwise be delayed while actual costs are accumulated. As noted in the exhibit, this process starts by creating an allocation rate that is then used to charge costs to jobs. This standard rate is generally based on historical records, so it should not be too far from an allocation rate based on actual costs. In a separate step (as noted by the dividing line in the exhibit), we then accumulate all the actual costs incurred, just as in Exhibit 1.3, and store them in the overhead cost pool. Next we subtract the total amount allocated using the standard allocation rate from the actual amount of overhead costs. There should be a difference between the two types of allocation, which must then be disposed of.

There are three ways to eliminate a variance between the standard and actual allocation totals. One approach, as noted in the lower left corner of Exhibit 1.4, is to charge the entire variance to the cost of goods sold. This is the easiest approach, but it may skew the total cost of goods sold unless the amount of the variance is relatively small. The next option, as shown in the bottom center of the exhibit, is to prorate the variance among the cost of goods sold, work-in-process inventory, and finished goods inventory, based on the ending balances in each account. This option is most useful for external financial statement reporting, where such allocations are required, and is only slightly more difficult to calculate than the direct charge-off to the cost-of-goods-sold option. The final option, as noted in the lower right corner of the exhibit, is to charge the variance to each job that was open during the period when the overhead costs were being accumulated. This method is by far the most labor-intensive since there may be many jobs to which the variance must be allocated. It is recommended only if it is important to have the highest possible level of job record accuracy or if the variance is so large that the other two methods will yield inaccurate reporting results. To calculate this allocation, costs are spread to jobs based on their use of whatever activity measures were originally compiled to allocate overhead costs to them.

The exhibits in this section show the general flow of transactions required to operate a job costing system. Though the basic steps are not difficult to follow, there are quite a few of them, which makes job costing a tricky system to operate and one that frequently results in odd-looking results, thereby forcing the cost accountant to engage in considerable account tracing and reconciliation to see where accounting transactions were incorrectly processed. To avoid these problems, anyone involved with job costing transactions should be thoroughly versed in the process flows noted here.

CONTROL POINT ISSUES

The job costing system requires a significant number of inputs, variance dispositions, and allocations and so is subject to problems at a number of control points. By being aware of these problems, one can revise the system to avoid control problems. This section contains a review of the most common issues.

Disposition of job costing variances is one of the most common control problems. If a manager is oriented toward improving reported profit levels (perhaps because his bonus would be increased), variances are never charged to the cost of goods sold even if they are due to abnormal scrap or spoilage situations. Instead, they are rolled into overhead or prorated among the period-end inventory and cost-of-goods-sold accounts, which keeps some of them from being recognized as expenses in the near term. The best solution to this problem is to periodically review the journal entries used to dispose of variances, as well as to investigate the nature of each one, which can be an ongoing task for the internal auditing department.

A manager who wants to increase profits also has an incentive to park as many jobs in work in process as possible, even if they have really been completed. This gives the manager one or more buckets in which to store extra costs that would otherwise be shifted to finished goods and from there to the cost of goods sold. One way to avoid this issue is to look for old jobs that have not yet been closed. However, a canny manager may shift costs from old jobs to newer ones as the old ones are closed, so it may also be necessary to look for transactions that shift costs between jobs.

Yet another way to pump up reported profit levels is to use indirect labor personnel for work that is really of the direct labor variety, so that these labor costs are shifted to an overhead cost pool rather than being charged straight to a job. If this is done, it is likely that some of the overhead costs will be stored in an inventory account at the end of the accounting period rather than being charged straight to the cost of goods sold. This practice can be avoided by running a trend line of direct labor costs to see if these costs are being reduced despite steady or upward trends in production volume.

An additional control problem occurs when a manager loads costs into a job not scheduled to be sold for some time, thereby keeping them from being charged to the cost of goods sold. This results in a bloated work-in-process or finished goods inventory. The best avoidance measure here is to compare actual job costs to budgeted levels to see if overages are occurring, especially if they are occurring on jobs that are not yet completed.

Another control problem is carrying job cost variances past the end of the fiscal year. A legitimate system always charges any remaining variances to the cost of goods sold. However, anyone wanting to increase reported profit levels tries to avoid this and so routes the variances into an inventory account, thereby hopefully escaping the attention of the auditors who review the year-end accounting records. Once the auditors are gone, the variance is taken back out of the inventory account and charged off in the next year. This issue requires a close examination of the variance accounts to see what journal entries are made to reduce variance levels. If there are many entries running in and out of these accounts, it can be quite a chore to spot such transactions.

Another control problem involves someone trying to add costs to overhead cost pools that are really period expenses and should therefore be charged to the current period. When they are stored in the overhead cost pool, some portion of the overhead is stored in inventory instead of being expensed, thereby increasing reported profits. This common problem can be detected by periodically tracing the origins of all costs added to cost pools, as well as by running trend lines of cost pool totals just to see if they are on a steadily increasing path (which may indicate the addition of unrelated costs).

Another problem arises in the area of allocation methodology. The most appropriate way to spread costs to jobs may be through a number of cost pools and allocation methods (such as through an activity-based costing system), which yields the most accurate allocations. If this is not done, perhaps through the excessive accumulation of costs into too few cost pools or through inappropriate allocation techniques, the amount of overhead costs charged to each job may be too low or too high. This issue can be avoided by using an activity-based costing system.

When there are many product lines in a facility, it is also possible that different job costing systems are set up for each one because different costing personnel are used to create each one or because there is some perceived justification for using different cost accumulation or allocation systems. In reality this creates confusion, leading to inefficient costing systems. It is better to force all production lines into the same job costing mold.

Allocations can be inaccurate if a company chooses to use a normal costing system without some historical basis for using standard costs. When this happens, the allocations vary significantly from actual costs, resulting in repeated adjustments to the allocation rates being used, which in turn results in inaccurate overhead costs being assigned to jobs. In such situations it is better to start with an overhead allocation system based on actual costs and then switch over to a normal costing system *after* there is a history of costs on which to base a set of valid overhead standards.

A final problem is that some companies feel compelled to update their cost allocation rates too frequently, perhaps every month. They may do this based on a feeling that allocation rates are not accurate if they are not regularly compared to actual costs. However, there can be considerable fluctuation in monthly costs, based on seasonal cost changes, based on the number of workdays in each month, or because the accounts payable staff erroneously records no expenses in one month and double the amount in the next month. Whatever the reason, it is common to see costs fluctuate from month to month, which results in allocation rates for jobs that fluctuate in a corresponding manner. It is better to wait a few months before updating allocation rates simply because a longer time period flattens out any monthly cost changes.

Clearly, there are many control issues related to the job costing system. This does not mean that job costing is an inefficient system, just that it incorporates so many transactions that there are many situations in which costs can be deliberately or accidentally skewed. Thus, one must keep a watchful eye on the overall process in order to ensure that transactions are appropriately processed.

SUMMARY

Job costing is one of the primary cost tracking systems employed by corporations today. Because it is commonly used, the cost accountant will probably encounter the transactions described in the chapter at some point and so should know how to operate the system and have a firm grasp of its problems and control issues. Because this system is frequently used does not mean that it is perfectly suited to all situations, however; on the contrary, it is too much work for many cost accountants in relation to the types of information it produces. Consequently, one should review the other costing systems described in this book to see if one of them will work better or if job costing can be combined with a different costing system to yield the best blend of efficiency and effectiveness.

2

Process Costing

Process costing is used in many industries where there are such large quantities of similar products that it makes no sense to track the cost of either individual products or small batches of them. Instead, costs are averaged over large quantities of production, yielding the same unit costs for all items in a production run. This type of costing requires accounting calculations considerably different from those used for job costing in the last chapter, though the resulting transactions are similar. In this chapter we review the nature of process costing, the three most commonly used process costing calculations, and the advantages and disadvantages associated with this methodology.

NATURE OF PROCESS COSTING

Process costing is used in situations where job costing cannot be used; that is, for the mass production of similar products when the costs associated with individual units of output cannot be differentiated from each other. In other words, the cost of each product produced is assumed to be the same as the cost of every other product. Examples of industries where this type of production occurs include oil refining, food production, and chemical processing. For example, how would a cost accountant determine the precise cost required to create one gallon of aviation fuel when thousands of gallons of the same fuel are gushing out of a refinery every hour? The cost accounting methodology in this case is process costing.

    There are three types of process costing. The first is based on weighted average costs and is described in the next section. It assumes that all costs, whether from a preceding period or the current one, are lumped together and assigned to produced units. It is the simplest version to calculate. The second type of process costing is based on standard costs. Its calculation is similar to that for weighted average costing, but standard costs are assigned to production units rather than actual costs; after total costs are accumulated based on standard costs, these totals are compared to actual accumulated costs and the difference is charged to a variance account. This calculation is described in "Process Costing Data Flow, Standard Costing Method." Finally, one can use first-in first-out costing. This is a more complex calculation that creates layers of costs, one for units of production started in the previous production period but not completed, and another layer for production started in the current period. This calculation is described in "Process Costing Data Flow, the FIFO Method." For a more detailed review of the FIFO concept, the reader should refer to Chapter 5, which covers cost layering concepts. Anyone already familiar with these concepts might ask why no costing formulation is presented here for last-in first-out cost layering. The LIFO concept is used to determine the cost-of-finished-goods inventory in situations where the last units of inventory added to a stockpile are the first removed from the pile and sold. Though the LIFO concept is perfectly valid for final sales to customers, it is not a reasonable system to use within a company, where production moves through the facility in a steady stream—the first production unit to enter a department is also the first one to leave it. Since the theoretical LIFO concept is not actually encountered in the majority of production situations, we do not include a costing example based on it in this chapter.

Why have three different cost calculation methods for process costing, and why use one version instead of another? Different calculations are required for different cost accounting needs. The weighted average method is used in situations where there is no standard costing system or where the fluctuations in costs from period to period are so slight that the management team has no need for the slight improvement in costing accuracy that can be obtained with the FIFO costing method. Alternatively, process costing based on standard costs is required for costing systems that use standard costs. It is also useful in situations where companies manufacture such a broad mix of products that they have difficulty accurately assigning actual costs to each type of product; under the other process costing methodologies, which both use actual costs, there is a strong chance that costs for different products will become mixed together. Finally, FIFO costing is used when there are ongoing, significant changes in product costs from period to period—to such an extent that the management team needs to know the new costing levels so that it can reprice products appropriately, determine if there are internal costing problems requiring resolution, or perhaps change manager performance-based compensation. In general, the simplest costing approach is the weighted average method, with FIFO costing being the most difficult. If there are no other factors impacting one's decision regarding which method to use, it is best to stay with the simplest system.

PROCESS COSTING DATA FLOW, WEIGHTED AVERAGE METHOD

The weighted average method is the easiest process costing system to understand because it uses actual costs and does not attempt to create layers of costs, as is the case with the first-in first-out method (described later in this chapter). The method is best illustrated with an example, which is shown in Exhibit 2.1.

Two types of costs are assigned to products during a process costing calculation. One is direct materials, and the other is all other conversion costs required to complete the processing of the product; conversion costs can include labor, overhead charges, and so on. Direct materials are generally added at the beginning of the production process, while other conversion costs are more commonly added throughout the process. For example, a furniture maker starts with a block of wood and continually adds labor to it for the remainder of the production process in order to arrive at a completed wooden bureau—the direct materials are added at the beginning of the process, and the conversion costs are added in a steady stream. In our example we assume that costs are added to the process flow in this manner. In Exhibit 2.1, the top section is devoted to the calculation of units of production based on the concept that direct materials are completed first. In this section, "Units Summary," we see that the production process has successfully com-

Exhibit 2.1 Weighted Average Costing Method Example

Weighted Average Cost Allocation Method

Units Summary	Direct Material Units	Conversion Factor	Conversion Cost Units	
Completed Units	1,000		1,000	
		60%		
Ending Units in Process	350		210	
Unit Totals	1,350		1,210	

Unit Cost Calculation	Direct Materials		Conversion Costs	Totals
Beginning WIP Cost	$ 20,000		$ 15,000	$ 35,000
Current Period Costs	$ 28,000		$ 21,500	$ 49,500
Total Costs	$ 48,000		$ 36,500	$ 84,500
Unit Totals (see above)	1,350		1,210	
Cost per Unit	$ 35.556		$ 30.165	

Unit Cost Allocation	Direct Materials		Conversion Costs	Totals
Cost of Completed Units	$ 35,556		$ 30,165	$ 65,721
Cost of Ending WIP Units	$ 12,444		$ 6,335	$ 18,779
Totals	$ 48,000		$ 36,500	$ 84,500

pleted 1,000 units during the period. Since these units are fully completed and shipped out of the company, the number of units from the perspective of cost application is the same for both direct materials and conversion costs—1,000 units. However, there are also some units that were still in the production process at the end of the accounting period, totaling 350 units. The treatment of these units is somewhat different. From a cost application perspective, we assume that all 350 units are present for direct material cost application since all 350 units had all the direct materials added to them at the beginning of the process. However, conversion costs have been only partially applied. According to the production manager, only 60% of all conversion costs have been applied to these units as of the end of the accounting period. We enter this number in the "Conversion Factor" field and multiply it by the total of 350 units that were in process, which gives us just 210 units for purposes of conversion cost application. Thus, the weighted average cost allocation method yields 1,350 units of completed production for the purpose of applying direct material costs, but only 1,210 units for applying conversion costs.

Next we must determine the cost per unit. This calculation is shown in the middle of Exhibit 2.1 under "Unit Cost Calculation." In this section we enter the beginning work-in-process costs for both direct materials and conversion costs, which should be stored in the general ledger from the preceding accounting period. We then compile all costs added during the current period and enter them on the next line, which gives us total direct material costs of $48,000 and total conversion costs of $36,500, for a grand total of $84,500. We then enter the unit totals from the preceding section and divide them into the cost totals for direct materials and conversion costs, which yields a cost per unit of $35.556 for direct materials and $30.165 per unit for conversion costs.

Finally, we multiply the unit costs we have just calculated by the number of units of completed production and remaining work in process in order to determine which costs are assigned to the finished goods general ledger account and which to the work-in-process account. To do this, we proceed to the bottom of Exhibit 2.1 to the section "Unit Cost Allocation." There are four calculations in this section. To determine the amount of total direct materials to charge to the finished goods account, we multiply the completed units of 1,000 at the top of the exhibit by the cost per unit to arrive at a total of $35,556. Similarly, we multiply 1,000 completed units in the conversion cost column by the conversion cost per unit of $30.165 to arrive at a total conversion cost per completed unit of $30,165. This gives us a total completed unit cost of $65,721, as noted in the far-right column at the bottom of the page. We then perform the same calculations to determine the cost of the work-in-process inventory, but now we use units itemized under "Ending Units in Process" to perform the calculation with the same costs per unit. This results in total direct material costs of $12,444 and total conversion costs of $6,335, for a grand total of $18,779 being charged to the work-in-process inventory account. To assist in the understanding of these calculations, arrows have been inserted into the exhibit to give a visual reference to the flow of each calculation. As a check on our calculations, we can see that the $84,500 of total costs used in the center of the exhibit to determine the cost per unit is the same amount that we have arrived at in the bottom section, so all costs incurred are being charged to the general ledger inventory accounts.

The explanation for weighted average costing has been a lengthy one, yet it is the simplest of the three process costing variations described in this chapter. The main reason for the complicated calculations is the split between costs for direct materials and conversion costs. Why not just combine the two costs, thereby cutting the total number of calculations in half? The reason is that costs could then be significantly skewed. For example, if one were to assume that all conversion costs are assigned at the *beginning* of the production process, thereby avoiding the need for a conversion factor in Exhibit 2.1, there would be a resulting increase in the ending work-in-process valuation of about $3,000 and a drop in the finished goods valuation of the same amount. This may seem like a paltry change in the balances of the two inventory accounts, but what if all the finished goods are sold before the end of the accounting period? This would result in a $3,000 reduction in the cost of goods sold during the period, which would increase profits by a corresponding amount. This altered calculation is shown in Exhibit 2.2 with all changes noted in boldface.

As noted in Exhibit 2.2, we must separate the direct material cost and conversion cost calculations or run the risk of arriving at incorrect inventory valuation calculations that can result in an incorrect cost of goods sold.

PROCESS COSTING DATA FLOW, STANDARD COSTING METHOD

The costing solution noted in the last section may not be acceptable for companies that operate on a standard costing system

Exhibit 2.2 Costing Calculation with No Consideration of the Conversion Factor

Weighted Average Cost Allocation Method

Units Summary	Direct Material Units	Conversion Factor	Conversion Cost Units
Completed Units	1,000		1,000
		100%	
Ending Units in Process	350		350
Unit Totals	1,350		1,350

Unit Cost Calculation	Direct Materials		Conversion Costs	Totals
Beginning WIP Cost	$ 20,000		$ 15,000	$ 35,000
Current Period Costs	$ 28,000		$ 21,500	$ 49,500
Total Costs	$ 48,000		$ 36,500	$ 84,500
Unit Totals (see above)	1,350		1,350	
Cost per Unit	$ 35.556		$ 27.037	

Unit Cost Allocation	Direct Materials		Conversion Costs	Totals
Cost of Completed Units	$ 35,556		$ 27,037	$ 62,593
Cost of Ending WIP Units	$ 12,444		$ 9,463	$ 21,907
Totals	$ 48,000		$ 36,500	$ 84,500

Variance from Preceding Exhibit:	Preceding Exhibit Totals	This Exhibit Totals	Variance
Cost of Completed Units	$ 65,721	$ 62,593	$ 3,128
Cost of Ending WIP Units	$ 18,779	$ 21,907	$ (3,128)
Totals	$ 84,500	$ 84,500	$ -

(Chapter 4). These organizations use a standard, predetermined cost for each step in the production process and deal separately with any variances from these standards. We can accommodate these companies by altering the weighted average model from the last section so that standard costs are assigned instead of actual costs, with any differences being charged to variance accounts. This costing model is shown in Exhibit 2.3.

In the exhibit the numbers used are the same as in Exhibit 2.1, so that differences in calculations can be easily seen. The section "Unit Summary" at the top of the exhibit is identical to the format used for weighted average costing. The main difference is in the second section of the exhibit, where there is no calculation of total beginning work-in-process or current period costs, which are normally used to derive the cost per unit. Instead, preset standard costs are used. So far, this makes the calculations *easier* than in the weighted average model (though this soon changes). The next step is to assign the standard costs to the units of production, the calculation of which is identical to that in the weighted average costing system. At this point we would have completed our calculations for the weighted average model. Here, however, we must insert a fourth section into the model that summarizes actual costs during the period and subtracts them from the standard costs already calculated, yielding a variance for both direct materials and conversion costs. These variances are then charged to the cost of goods sold. This final step makes the standard costing method slightly more time-consuming than the weighted average method.

As noted in an earlier section, the standard costing approach is most useful for situations where a number of products are being manufactured, which increases the danger that the costs for different products will be mixed together, resulting in inaccurate product costing. By using standard instead of actual costs, a company can reliably assign costs to all products that are fully provable.

PROCESS COSTING DATA FLOW, THE FIFO METHOD

The final method for calculating process costs is the FIFO method. This is a cost layering approach that requires more calculations than

Exhibit 2.3 Standard Costing Method Example

Weighted Average Cost Allocation Method Using Standard Costs

Units Summary	Direct Material Units	Conversion Factor	Conversion Cost Units
Completed Units	1,000		1,000
		60%	
Ending Units in Process	350		210
Unit Totals	1,350		1,210

Unit Cost Calculation	Direct Materials		Conversion Costs
Standard Unit Cost	$ 32.000		$ 31.500

Unit Cost Allocation	Direct Materials		Conversion Costs	Totals
Standard Cost of Completed Units	$ 32,000		$ 31,500	$ 63,500
Standard Cost of Ending WIP Units	$ 11,200		$ 6,615	$ 17,815
Standard Costs Totals	$ 43,200		$ 38,115	$ 81,315

Period Variance				
Beginning Standard WIP Cost	$ 20,000		$ 15,000	$ 35,000
Current Period Actual Costs	$ 28,000		$ 21,500	$ 49,500
Total Period Costs	$ 48,000		$ 36,500	$ 84,500
Standard Cost Totals	$ 43,200		$ 38,115	$ 81,315
Cost Variance	$ 4,800		$ (1,615)	$ 3,185

the previous two methods. Once again, we illustrate the method with an example, as shown in Exhibit 2.4. In this instance we add extra calculations and separate the costs recorded in the general ledger for work-in-process units from the previous period.

In the example we no longer identify just the completed and work-in-process units of production in the "Units Summary" portion of

Exhibit 2.4 Process Costing Method Example

First-In First-Out Cost Allocation Method

Units Summary	Direct Material Units	Conversion Factor	Conversion Cost Units	Total Units
Units from Beginning WIP	-	75% [work not done]	225	300
New Units Finished in Period	700		700	700
Ending Units in Process	350	60% [work done]	210	350
Unit Totals	1,050		1,135	1,350

Unit Cost Calculation	Direct Materials		Conversion Costs	Totals
Current Period Costs	$ 28,000		$ 21,500	$ 49,500
Unit Totals (see above)	$ 1,050		$ 1,135	
Costs per Unit	$ 26.667		$ 18.943	

Unit Cost Allocation	Direct Materials		Conversion Costs	Totals
Beginning Work-in-Process Cost	$ 20,000		$ 15,000	$ 35,000
Costs Added to Beginning WIP Units	$ -		$ 4,262	$ 4,262
Costs Added to New Units Finished in Period	$ 18,667		$ 13,260	$ 31,927
Costs Added to Ending Work in Process	$ 9,333		$ 3,978	$ 13,311
Totals	$ 48,000		$ 36,500	$ 84,500

the spreadsheet. Instead, we also separate the units that were in the work-in-process account at the end of the preceding period. By doing so, we can segregate the cost of work done in the previous period, which may be different from the costs per unit incurred in the current period. The result of this additional segregation in production units is that the unit totals are now lower, with only 1,050 units appearing for direct material costing purposes and 1,135 for conversion costing purposes. This is because we have split the 1,000 completed units itemized in the preceding examples into 300 units that were not completed in the previous period and 700 units that were both started and completed in the current period. The FIFO system records units for costing purposes in the current period only if there are additional costs that must be added to the units. Accordingly, zero direct material units are shown in the "Units from Beginning WIP" row since the direct material costs were all added in the previous period. However, 75% of the conversion work has not yet been done on these units (as noted in the same row), so 75% of the 300 units (225 units) are shown in the "Conversion Cost Units" category. All other parts of the "Units Summary" portion of the analysis remain the same.

Next we move to the "Unit Cost Calculation" portion of the exhibit. Here we see that only costs incurred in the current period are used to calculate the cost per unit. The reason for excluding the cost of incoming work in process for the preceding period is that we are attempting to create a cost layer specific to the units of production in the current period *only*. The costs stored in inventory at the end of the preceding accounting period have not gone away but have just shifted to the "Unit Cost Allocation" section of the exhibit. Meanwhile, we calculate the cost per unit in the usual manner, obtaining a direct material cost per unit of $26.667 and a conversion cost per unit of $18.943. These unit costs are lower than the costs derived for the weighted average and standard costing methods because we have thus far excluded costs from the beginning work-in-process inventory. Once these costs are added back in (in the last part of the exhibit), we will see that all costs have been accounted for.

Finally, we must complete the "Unit Cost Allocation" at the bottom of the exhibit, which tells us what costs to assign to either finished goods or work-in-process inventory. First, we add all beginning work-in-process costs, which are shown in the first row. Next we add to them any additional costs incurred during the current period in order to complete units of production started in the previous reporting period. To do this, we multiply the units in the "Units from Beginning WIP" row at the top of the exhibit by the unit cost. This results in no additional cost allocation for direct materials but in an extra $4,262 of conversion costs. At this point we have completed the costing for all the units of production started but not completed in the preceding period, which totals $39,262. This cost is then shifted to the finished goods account in the general ledger. Next we multiply the production units that were both started and completed in the current period by the cost per unit, which results in total direct material costs of $18,667 and conversion costs of $13,260. These costs are also shifted to the finished goods account. Finally, we multiply the ending units in process quantities by the unit costs to derive the cost totals that will be transferred to the work-in-process inventory account in the general ledger. These costs are $9,333 for direct materials and $3,978 for conversion costs, for a total ending work-in-process cost of $13,311. Six calculations are required to determine the numbers in the "Unit Cost Allocation" section, so arrows have been added to ease the task of tracing the flow of each one. Also, note that the total amount allocated is $84,500 (as shown in the lower right corner of the exhibit), which proves that we have allocated all the costs with which we started the calculation.

In essence, we have segregated the cost of work done in the previous period, added any costs incurred in the current period to complete unfinished work from the previous period, and run a separate set of calculations to charge costs to all other units of production that are based on costs incurred in the current period. Thus, we have effectively avoided merging costs from different periods. This does not have a large impact on a company's reported costs as long as costs do not vary much from period to period. However, if costs fluctuate considerably over time, it may make sense to use this more complicated calculation to ensure that cost changes are immediately reflected in the financial statements of the period in which they occurred.

ADVANTAGES AND DISADVANTAGES OF PROCESS COSTING

Process costing is the only reasonable approach to determining product costs in many industries. From the three costing methodologies just described in this chapter, a company can select the best one for determining costs in either a standard or actual costing environment. Process costing also uses most of the same journal entries found in a job costing environment, so there is no need to restructure the chart of accounts to any significant degree. This makes it easy to switch over to a job costing system from a process costing one if the need arises, or to adopt a hybrid approach that uses parts of both systems.

Despite these advantages there are several problems with process costing that one should be aware of. The most obvious is determining the percentage of completion. This percentage is needed to calculate the amount of costs to be assigned to units of production in each period. If the percentage is incorrect, resulting unit valuations will also be wrong. A canny manager aware of this problem can manipulate the percentage of completion to raise or lower unit costs, thereby changing the reported level of profitability. This problem is difficult to sidestep if the manager causing the trouble is in a position of authority. If not, cross-checking of completion percentages can be used to introduce some accuracy verification. Another solution is to establish a preset completion percentage, such as 50%, that is never changed in any reporting period no matter what the actual level of completion is. Unfortunately, this option can lead to manipulation also, for a manager could dump partially completed products into a department just to have extra costs automatically charged to that department, or arbitrarily held in an upstream department, depending on what types of cost results are desired. A further option is to divide conversion costs into several cost pools, rather than one large cost pool, and separately determine the percentage of completion for each one, with a different person responsible for each determination. Though this approach can result in more accurate overall estimates, it is also a more complicated system to maintain.

Another problem arises with transfer costs if any of these process costing methodologies are used for individual departments. The trouble is that each successive department inherits the entire costs from the preceding set of departments that have charged costs to the products being manufactured and so has no idea which portion of the incoming costs are variable and which are overhead allocations. It is important to know the variable portion of one's costs since they can be used for incremental pricing decisions. The best way to avoid this difficulty is to use process costing only for the company as a whole, rather than for each of a series of departments, so that variable costs (e.g., direct material costs) can be more readily split off from the total costs. However, this is not possible in companies with long production cycles because process costs are spread over many units of production in many stages of completion, resulting in inaccurate per-unit costs.

Another difficulty is associated with the chart of accounts. Though the journal entries related to process costing are similar to those used for job costing, there is one difference. Job costing assigns costs to specific jobs within the work-in-process inventory account, whereas costs in a process costing environment can be shifted from department to department as products move through the production process. Thus, the focus of data collection shifts from jobs to departments. This change requires the addition of one or more digits to each account number in the chart of accounts, which identifies each department.

A problem specific to the weighted average calculation with standard costing is the deliberate alteration of standard costs in order to create variances. If a manager wants to create an accounting profit in a given period, he can order the standard costs for products to be produced in the current period to be set somewhat high. In this way additional direct materials and conversion costs are stored in inventory. This variance results in a false increase in the reported level of profitability, a problem that can be partly corrected by giving the engineering staff tight control over standard cost changes. Nonetheless, someone at the level of general manager could still muster sufficient authority to overcome such controls.

Of the issues noted here the primary one is incorrect estimation of the percentage of completion. Consequently, the bulk of the cost accountant's efforts in this area should be directed toward creating a solid estimating system not subject to coercion.

SUMMARY

Process costing is a common cost summarization and allocation methodology, three variations of which are most heavily used. It tends to be a relatively inexpensive system to operate but also runs the risk of producing inaccurate outputs, especially if a company's systems are a mixture of job- and process-based production. Consequently one should carefully consider how this system fits into existing production systems and what special cost system alterations are required to ensure that the collected data can be converted to the most useful set of costing information.

3

Direct Costing

Direct costing is either highly favored or much maligned by cost accountants; those who favor it claim that it is helpful for a number of short-term decisions, while those against it point out that it does not include many of the costs to which today's overhead-heavy firms are subjected, and thereby leads to poor decisions. In this chapter we explore the nature of direct costing and how it can be used to improve management decision making. We also note its flaws and how to avoid them. Finally, we present brief discussions of what happens to financial reporting and inventory valuation when direct costing is used in their compilation.

DEFINITION OF DIRECT COSTING

There are several ways to define direct costs, so rather than create an amalgamated definition, we list several distinct ones:

- ○ All costs left after period-specific costs have been eliminated
- ○ All costs that can be directly attributed to an incremental change in production volume
- ○ All costs that can be reasonably allocated to specific units of production
- ○ All costs that would disappear if the related production volume were to stop

Though these definitions appear to be somewhat different, a common thread runs through them all—a direct cost must be one that is clearly attached to incremental changes in production volume. That is, the cost changes if the volume changes.

The obvious costs that can be readily considered direct costs are those for materials and direct labor used to construct a product or provide a service. There are a number of other lesser costs that can sometimes be added to these two major costs, such as the payroll taxes that accompany direct labor and incidental supplies needed to construct a product. For example, the bill of materials for a product may not include the cost of fittings or fasteners because corporate policy charges these costs to expense in each period under the category "shop supplies." Nonetheless, these costs are consumed during the manufacture of the product and are therefore direct costs.

The list of costs that can be considered direct costs changes as the volume of production increases. For example, when a cost accountant is reviewing an issue related to the incremental pricing of one additional unit of production, its direct cost is just its material cost since the direct labor staff is not sent home just to avoid the hours required to make one extra unit (assuming a small amount of labor per unit). Under this scenario the amount of direct labor cost goes down as the related unit volume decreases. However, when the same product is analyzed in terms of an entire batch of production, the direct costs include the cost of utilities incurred by any machines involved in the batch processing, as well as the cost of any labor needed to set up or break down the machinery for a production run. At high volume levels, direct costs can include the cost of an entire factory. Consequently, which costs to include in the direct cost category vary directly with the production volume addressed by the analysis being made.

Direct costs can also switch to being indirect ones (and vice versa), depending on management decisions. For example, if a company has a labor-intensive production process and management decides to switch its production process over to one that replaces much of the direct labor with automated machinery, the direct cost of each incremental unit of production declines by the cost of the direct labor that has been eliminated, while the period costs, which now include the cost of the automated machinery, increase.

Having noted that costs defined as direct vary based on the circumstances, we bring up the question of how a cost accountant is supposed to know when a cost is direct and when it is not. There are three ways to make this distinction. The first is to use one's judgment. As noted in the next section, the primary use of direct costing is for short-term, incremental decisions related to pricing, product mix, and contribution margins. Given these uses, the cost accountant must determine the production volume being considered in each individual analysis and use her knowledge of the company's costs to determine which ones should be classified as direct for the purposes of that analysis. Since this may require some specialized knowledge of how costs are incurred, the cost accountant should feel free to call on internal experts in company operations, such as industrial engineers or shift managers, for advice on how to classify costs. This is a quick and relatively accurate way to determine the nature of a cost and is the method most frequently used, especially when there is little time for either of the other two methods.

An alternative approach is to rely on the industrial engineering staff to conduct an engineering review of how each cost is incurred and what activities cause it to be incurred. Though an accurate approach, this is by far the most labor-intensive way to determine the nature of a cost and so is rarely used for ongoing cost accounting analyses.

The final method for determining a direct cost is through the use of statistical analysis. Regression analysis can be used to determine the "best fit" line that plots a set of costs at various levels of a supposedly related activity. When the slope of this line is steep, there is clearly a close relationship between the activity and the cost. For example, there is an obviously tight relationship between the cost of materials and production volume, whereas the cost of supervisory salaries and the level of production are not closely linked. Though this method requires less time to complete than an engineering study, it is still substantially longer than the first method and so is used only for the most detailed cost accounting analyses where a high degree of precision is required.

Now that we have a clear conception of a direct cost, what about all the costs that are *not* direct? How are they classified? These costs are known as period costs since their incurrence bears no relationship to future activities that fall outside the current accounting period. Examples of these costs are administrative salaries, research and development, machinery depreciation, maintenance, and utilities—essentially all the categories of overhead or general and administrative expenses that cannot be directly assigned to the manufacture of individual units of production.

Another way of looking at these period costs is to think of them as the cost of capacity during the period. They must be incurred in order to keep a company ready to fill a customer order, even if that order never arrives. When period costs are interpreted in this manner, management's attention is focused on whether or not it should maintain the current level of capacity. If it wishes to reduce period costs, then a likely result will be a diminution in the company's ability to process the same level of transactions; this may be acceptable if a smaller level of production is needed to fill customer orders.

The final element in the definition of a direct cost is the contribution margin. This is simply revenues minus direct costs. It is not the same as the gross margin, which requires the inclusion of all related overhead costs in its calculation, whereas the contribution margin calculation specifically excludes overhead costs. Consequently, the contribution margin is always higher than the gross margin. Its use is described in the next section.

The key points in this section were descriptions of direct costs, period costs, and the contribution margin, which are the primary components of the analyses discussed in the next section. It is also important to note that, because direct costing involves only a subset of a company's total costs, it is not a system that one should rely on for all of a company's costing needs. It is useful only for specific purposes, which will be defined in the next section.

USES OF DIRECT COSTING

Direct costing is used for a limited set of cost accounting analyses because it does not consider overhead (period) costs. However, the uses to which it can be put are the ones most commonly encountered by the cost accountant, and so it is still a valuable tool. In this section we describe how direct costing can be used. Examples of the various types of analyses are:

○ **Which customers are most (un)profitable?** The majority of period costs bear no direct relationship to the costs incurred to service a specific customer, with a few exceptions, such as the cost of customer service, order taking, and shipment. Given the small number of costs involved, it is typically a simple matter to derive a customer profitability profile, such as the one noted in Exhibit 3.1, which summarizes all customer revenues and related direct costs, to arrive at contribution margins by customer. In the exhibit it is evident that the profitability of sales to customer Q is quite low because of high labor and order taking costs (which are classic signs of a customer who requires an excessive degree of support). Management can use this information to determine which customers should be charged more in order to increase profits or dropped entirely so that available capacity can be used to sell to other, more profitable customers. The same format can also be used to determine the profitability of entire sales regions, individual products, or product lines.

○ **What impact will automation have on our cost structure?** When automation is used to eliminate direct labor, the direct cost to produce an item inevitably goes down (since the direct labor element is reduced or eliminated), while the period cost goes up because of the increased cost of depreciation for the new equipment, as well as maintenance costs to keep it operational. From the perspective of direct costing, this means that a company has

Exhibit 3.1 Profitability by Customer, Using Direct Costs

	Customer B	Customer Q	Customer Z
Revenue ($)	12,598	23,042	100,782
Direct costs			
Materials ($)	6,250	11,500	51,432
Direct labor ($)	1,231	4,803	9,078
Commission of 5% ($)	630	1,152	5,039
Order taking cost ($)	126	3,050	1,008
Shipping cost ($)	252	461	2,016
Total direct costs ($)	8,489	20,966	68,573
Contribution margin ($)	4,109	2,076	32,209
Contribution margin (%)	33	1	32

a smaller incremental cost of production and can sell at an even lower price and still turn a profit. However, this lower price must still generate a sufficient contribution margin to ensure that period costs are covered.

○ **What profit can we expect at various volume levels?** Direct costing is very good for profitability modeling. As noted in Exhibit 3.2, one can set up a chart itemizing various levels of sales volume and calculate the direct costs for each one. Then the period costs, which are assumed to be constant, are added, resulting in estimated levels of profit.

○ **Can I use direct costing for make-or-buy decisions?** This is an excellent use for the direct costing methodology, for only direct costs should be included in the make-or-buy analysis. If a company needs to decide if it should manufacture a product in-house, versus at a supplier, most overhead costs are considered sunk costs that do not affect the decision. This leaves just the costs that will disappear if a product is removed from the production line and given to a supplier. This decision is described in greater detail in the case study at the end of this chapter.

○ **Can I use direct costing as the foundation for commission calculations?** Most commission systems are based on paying a percentage of a product's sale price to a salesperson after a sales

Exhibit 3.2 Profitability Analysis at Different Volume Levels

	Number of Units		
	10,000	20,000	30,000
Direct cost/unit ($)	17.43	17.43	17.43
Price/unit ($)	50.00	50.00	50.00
Total revenue ($)	500,000	1,000,000	1,500,000
Total direct cost ($)	174,300	348,600	522,900
Total period cost ($)	300,000	300,000	300,000
Profit (loss) ($)	25,700	351,400	677,100
Profit (%)	5	35	45

transaction has been completed. However, this method does not factor in the possibility that salespeople are selling whatever products are easiest for them to sell, rather than those with the highest level of profitability, which can result in massive sales of the wrong products and no bottom-line profits. To avoid this problem a company can alter the commission calculation system so that commissions are based on a product's contribution margin. Each product's standard contribution margin can be calculated once a year, and a standard commission payment generated based on this amount, which sales personnel will be awarded for selling each incremental unit of the product. Using the contribution margin as the basis for commission payments has the unique advantage of making it easy to explain to the sales staff, which may have a difficult time understanding how overhead costs can be applied to products.

○ **Can I determine which product sales yield the highest profit mix when capacity is fully utilized?** When companies find that there are more customer orders on hand than they can possibly fill given the constraints of production capacity, they are left with the problem of which orders to turn away. Direct costing can be used to decide which orders are the least and most profitable so that management can pick and choose among them, maximizing the total amount of profit earned. However, "cherry picking" among customer orders may permanently turn away some customers, which can be a major problem if the company later experiences a drop in orders and has alienated too many customers to regain sales volume.

In addition to the specific issues mentioned here, there are also some general benefits associated with the use of direct costing. One is that users can make fast analysis calculations, for there are so few costs associated with the direct costing system that they are easy to assemble. This is in opposition to an analysis that uses full-absorption costing, where one must not only determine the correct amount of overhead costs to allocate but also field questions from users regarding the applicability of these overhead allocations to the analysis in question.

Another point in its favor is that it is easy for users to understand. Any direct costing analysis is extremely simple, with only a few costs listed along with a contribution margin—there is no allocation of general and administrative costs, no overhead charge from corporate headquarters, and no allocation of costs from any number of cost pools. Many of the recipients of direct costing information are located in the sales and marketing department, where employees are highly trained in areas other than accounting and do not have time to puzzle over allocation rates and absorption levels. They are greatly appreciative of the clarity of direct costing and how it can help them in setting short-term pricing levels.

It is evident that direct costing is of great value in making a number of incremental pricing and costing decisions. However, the initial enthusiasm for this technique must be tempered by a knowledge of its pitfalls, which are described in the next section.

PROBLEMS WITH DIRECT COSTING

The single largest problem with direct costing is that it ignores all indirect costs. Though these costs may appear to be irrelevant in short-term decision making, which is where direct costing works best, they are still costs that must be factored into a company's long-range profitability planning. For example, when any of a company's indirect costs are treated by a direct costing analysis as though they do not exist, short-term pricing decisions that cover direct costs but most certainly do not cover indirect costs may result. When the company continues to use direct costing as its primary method for determining prices, it runs the risk of accepting margins that are much too low to pay for all the indirect company costs not included in the direct costing analysis. This is a serious problem for organizations, such as software companies, whose costs are almost entirely related to overhead. For example, the direct cost of selling one additional unit of software is only the cost of the CD or floppy disk on which it is stored (and not even that if the software is downloaded from a web site); a direct costing analysis for this type of product results in a recommendation to sell the software for almost no price at all, which would never come close to paying for all the associated overhead costs. Thus, an exclusive focus on short-term decisions, with direct costing serving as the basis for these decisions, can place a company in serious financial difficulty.

Another problem is that direct costing does not yield valid infor-

mation when it is used to analyze cases that fall outside the current capacity situation. For example, a sales manager is considering a proposal by a customer to purchase an additional 10,000 units of Product
Alpha. The direct costing analysis reveals that, at a price of $18 each,
the company will realize a profit of $2 per unit, or $20,000. However,
what the direct costing analysis does not show is that this proposal requires more production capacity than the company has available, so
that extra overtime, costing $22,000, or the addition of more auto-
mated machinery, costing three times the amount of the profits from
this prospective deal, will be required. In other words, direct costing
does not consider the additional cost of capacity that must be added if
an incremental pricing decision cannot be filled with the existing capacity. This shortcoming can be reduced by using expert opinion
and/or a review by the industrial engineering staff to determine the
added cost of any required capacity.

Another issue is that costs can switch between direct and indirect
costs for a number of reasons, which must be carefully investigated
when conducting a direct costing analysis. For example, the cost of
utilities is generally considered an indirect cost but can be defined as
a direct one when it is tracked for specific machines used in the production process. If such a machine is in operation to manufacture
goods, then the associated utility costs are clearly a direct cost. Similarly, if the chart of accounts is structured so that indirect costs are
coded for one specific manager and direct costs are coded for another (e.g., the vice president of administration and the vice president of production), shifting a cost to the responsibility of the person
in the indirect costing area can convert a direct cost to an indirect
one in the company's accounting system.

Another issue to be aware of is that the costs included in a direct
costing analysis gradually increase as the volume of production included in the analysis goes up. For example, when the subject of an
analysis is to produce only one extra unit of production, the only relevant cost is probably the associated material cost, and such a small
change in unit volume does not even have an impact on the company's ability to reduce the amount of direct labor employed during
the shift. However, when the unit volume included in the analysis increases, the ability to exclude or include additional direct labor is
relevant to the analysis. At larger volume levels the cost of the use of

specific machines, or of entire production lines, can be considered a direct cost. At high production volumes, the entire cost of a production facility can reasonably be considered direct costs. This is not really a problem with direct costing, but one must be aware of which costs are impacted by the production volumes considered during specific direct costing analyses—ignorance of this issue may result in the wrong costs being added to or excluded from a direct cost analysis.

The main point of this discussion is that direct costing is most relevant within a relatively narrow band of production volumes. As the number of units of production covered by an analysis mounts, one must continually verify that the set of costs identified for the analysis as being direct have not expanded to include additional costs that would otherwise be considered indirect.

USING DIRECT COSTING FOR COST CONTROL

Direct costing can be of great use in controlling costs, so much so that some organizations have converted their entire internal cost control systems to a direct costing basis.

The chief benefit of direct costing in the control of costs is that volume-based costs are split away from period costs so that each can be compared to budgeted cost levels in a different manner. For example, direct costs should be itemized on a per-unit budgeted cost basis and multiplied by the number of units manufactured to arrive at the budgeted total direct cost that should apply to a specific volume of production. An example of this is shown in Exhibit 3.3. This

Exhibit 3.3 Cost Control Report for Direct Costs

Actual Volume Produced: 13,412			
	Actual Cost ($)	Budgeted Cost ($)	Variance ($)
Direct material unit cost	14.02	14.00	−0.02
Direct labor unit cost	3.12	3.00	−0.12
Direct other unit cost	4.00	3.50	−0.50
Total direct unit cost	21.14	20.50	−0.64
Extended total direct cost	283,530	274,946	8,584

format is necessary because direct costs vary directly with volume, whereas period costs do not. Note in the example how there is no variance for the *volume* of production in this format since the budget is based on the cost per unit rather than the quantity produced.

Period costs are best compared to a fixed budget level for each period in the format shown in Exhibit 3.4. There is no need to convey to the reader what the production volume was in the period since the same cost amounts are incurred no matter what volume was generated. This is the standard format used for *all* costs by most companies but is really usable only when comparing period costs to a fixed budget.

Also, there may be a few costs that increase only when certain volume levels are reached, in a step-cost fashion. These require a mixed budget/actual reporting format, such as the one in Exhibit 3.5. This format allows the reader to select the most appropriate column of budgeted costs, based on actual production volume, and compare it to the actual costs column to see how well costs were controlled during the period. Note that this report contains no variance column. Given the large number of budget columns that address the costs at different activity levels, it would require many extra columns to detail the variances from actual for each one, so the report reader is left to determine the correct variance on her own.

Instead of using the cost control reports presented here, many companies use one report format for all three types of costs. Then it becomes nearly impossible to determine how well costs have been

Exhibit 3.4 Cost Control Report for Period Costs

	Actual Cost ($)	Budgeted Cost ($)	Variance ($)
Auditing fees	35,000	35,000	0
Insurance	5,400	5,000	−400
Legal fees	13,098	13,000	−98
Salaries, administration	207,892	210,000	2,108
Salaries, supervisory	78,045	82,000	3,955
Security services	3,742	2,500	−1,242
Total	**343,177**	**347,500**	**4,323**

Exhibit 3.5 Cost Control Report for Mixed Costs

	Actual Cost ($)	Budgeted Volume of 10,000 Units ($)	Budgeted Volume of 20,000 Units ($)	Budgeted Volume of 30,000 Units ($)
Production Volume: 23,200				
Maintenance	100,405	80,000	100,000	120,000
Production scheduling labor	48,250	45,000	47,500	50,000
Purchasing salaries	81,000	72,000	85,000	98,000
Utilities	71,381	48,000	60,000	72,000
Workers' compensation	14,501	12,000	15,000	18,000
Total	**315,537**	**257,000**	**307,500**	**358,000**

controlled since there is no way to relate production volumes to costs. In addition, this merged format typically calls for the allocation of overhead costs, which shifts costs from the period cost category to the direct cost area; as a result, these costs are so commingled that it is difficult to determine when or why costs were incurred or what budget they related to. This format is of little use to managers who want to know how well their company is controlling costs.

Consequently, it is clear that the more detailed set of reports shown here, which is based on the direct costing method, provides management with much better information for control purposes than the traditional single report that combines a number of different types of costs and then worsens matters by shuffling costs around under the guise of overhead allocation.

IMPACT OF DIRECT COSTING ON REPORTED FINANCIAL RESULTS

Direct costing is not allowed when reporting financial results to external entities, such as the investing public or creditors. However, it is frequently used in some capacity for internal management reports.

In this section we discuss how its use impacts the reported level of profitability, as well as how it can best be used.

One type of financial report is a comparison of budgeted to actual costs, which was covered in the last section. From that discussion it is apparent that using direct costing to divide costs into different types of variance reports makes it easier to see if a company is controlling its costs. Additional benefits are derived by not obscuring the expense line items by reallocating costs among them.

A different type of financial report is the format most commonly seen in external financial reports where revenues and expenses are compared to the results from previous reporting periods. If these reports are constructed with absorption costing, it is quite likely that a large number of costs will be carried over from month to month, on the assumption that they must be matched to revenues that have not yet occurred. In this way, the period-to-period financial results appear to be smoothed out—there are no sudden spikes in expenses. A different result appears when direct costing is used to create financial statements. In this case all period costs are expensed at once, rather than carrying them forward to a future period. This results in a uniform set of period expenses incurred in each reporting period, on the assumption that these costs are truly fixed or semifixed. When there are capacity costs associated with production, these costs are also charged to the current period rather than being rolled into the cost of finished goods or work in process. Accordingly, there are sudden jumps and dips in the reported level of profitability, depending on the amount of sales completed during the reporting period. An example is shown in Exhibits 3.6 and 3.7; the first exhibit shows a financial report that utilizes absorption costing, while the second reports the same financial and production volume information but uses direct costing principles. Note how the profitability level remains relatively steady from period to period in Exhibit 3.6 but varies widely in Exhibit 3.7.

The only difference in the information presented in the two exhibits is that Exhibit 3.6 shows the cost of overhead at a standard rate of $4.00 per unit sold, with any difference between this amount and the actual cost of overhead being rolled into the cost of inventory, which is presented at the bottom of the exhibit. The direct costing format in Exhibit 3.7 dispenses with this approach, instead electing

Exhibit 3.6 Financial Reporting with Absorption Costing

	Period 1	Period 2	Period 3
Units produced	50,000	50,000	50,000
Units sold	40,000	60,000	30,000
Price per unit ($)	28.00	28.00	28.00
Direct cost per unit ($)	15.00	15.00	15.00
Standard overhead cost per unit ($)	4.00	4.00	4.00
Actual overhead cost/period ($)	200,000	200,000	200,000
Revenue ($)	1,120,000	1,680,000	840,000
Cost of goods sold			
Materials and labor ($)	600,000	900,000	450,000
Overhead (at standard) ($)	160,000	240,000	120,000
Total cost of goods sold ($)	760,000	1,140,000	570,000
Gross margin ($)	360,000	540,000	270,000
Sales and administrative costs ($)	225,000	225,000	225,000
Profit (loss) ($)	135,000	315,000	45,000
Profit (loss) (%)	12	19	5
Overhead capitalized into inventory ($)	40,000	−40,000	80,000

Exhibit 3.7 Financial Reporting with Direct Costing

	Period 1	Period 2	Period 3
Units produced	50,000	50,000	50,000
Units sold	40,000	60,000	30,000
Price per unit ($)	28.00	28.00	28.00
Direct cost per unit ($)	15.00	15.00	15.00
Standard overhead cost per unit ($)	4.00	4.00	4.00
Actual overhead cost/period ($)	200,000	200,000	200,000
Revenue ($)	1,120,000	1,680,000	840,000
Cost of goods sold			
Materials and labor ($)	600,000	900,000	450,000
Overhead (at actual) ($)	200,000	200,000	200,000
Total cost of goods sold ($)	800,000	1,100,000	650,000
Gross margin ($)	320,000	580,000	190,000
Sales and administrative costs ($)	225,000	225,000	225,000
Profit (loss) ($)	$95,000	$355,000	$35,000
Profit (loss) (%)	8	21	−4
Overhead capitalized into inventory ($)	0	0	0

to charge all current overhead costs to expense within the current period. As a result, the profitability level in the first exhibit has a high-low range of 14% and always shows a profit, whereas the second (direct costing) exhibit reveals a high-low profitability range of 25% and shows a loss in the final accounting period. These radical differences in reported results are due solely to the treatment of overhead costs.

The erratic financial results of the direct costing method do not mean that it creates incorrect results—on the contrary, an examination of the cash flow statement for the same period would reveal that the direct costing method closely mirrors the actual cash flows of the company. Since there are no allocations or capitalizations of costs under the direct costing methodology, it closely reflects how cash actually moves through a company. If these cash flows happen to be erratic, then so be it—the system shows how the company actually operates.

Another reason why the financial results reported under direct costing are better than those using absorption costing is that the information presented yields more accurate trend lines of costs incurred. For example, if a manager wants to know the cost of machine maintenance incurred over a series of consecutive reporting periods, he might have a difficult time obtaining this information under an absorption costing system. The cost may have been rolled into a machine cost pool and then further allocated to the cost of production or capitalized into inventory—which can be a tortuous path to retrace to find out the monthly cost incurred. Direct costing, however, leaves costs in the accounts in which they were first incurred, so that it is a simple matter to accumulate costs and create trend lines that are accurate over long periods of time.

Another reason for using direct costing for financial reports is that it can be used to create rapid estimates of period profits. This is easy because the information is so clearly laid out, with no allocations between expense accounts or costs being capitalized into (or out of) inventory. A financial statement based on absorption costing, however, would require considerable amounts of investigation before its information could be used as the foundation for a financial analysis.

An unusual reason for using direct costing instead of absorption costing for financial statements is that statements based on absorption costing do not yield costs that are quite so smooth from period to period as one might think. The reason for this is that costs in each period that cannot be charged to the current period (because of excessive volumes of production) are charged instead to inventory or (less directly) to a volume variance account itemized on the balance sheet as inventory; from time to time, the amount of costs charged to inventory or a volume variance are reviewed, and any excessive amounts are charged to the current period if the amount of inventory on hand no longer justifies the capitalization of so many costs. When this charge-off occurs, there is a sudden spike in costs, which skews the reported level of profitability for the period. This charge-off has more to do with the timing of accounting staff reviews of capitalized expenses than with any particular volume of production, so it cannot be explained by changes in the activity level of the company. Also, because the analysis tends to be a complicated one, any related charge-off is also difficult to explain to nonaccountants. Thus, though direct costing has a reputation for resulting in highly variable financial results, the same can be said for absorption costing.

A final argument in favor of direct costing for financial reporting is the theory that many overhead costs are more closely related to a facility's available capacity than to the manufacture of additional units of capacity. Based on this theory, there should certainly be fewer overhead costs capitalized into inventory than is currently the case under absorption costing, and perhaps the same number as under direct costing (which is to say, none at all).

This discussion strongly favors the use of direct costing for financial reporting, but the one clear issue running against it is GAAP—this method is not allowable for external financial reporting. Though this view may change in the future, it is current practice, and so the use of direct costing must perforce be confined to reports intended strictly for internal consumption.

IMPACT OF DIRECT COSTING ON INVENTORY VALUATION

Direct costing is not allowed for the valuation of inventory under generally accepted accounting principles. The reason for this is that direct costing assumes that all period costs are charged to expense during the period, whereas GAAP state that some period costs directly tied to the production process should be allocated to any incremental increase in inventory that occurs during the period. If direct costing were used instead of this cost absorption method (which is still possible for internal accounting purposes), there would be differences in the cost of goods sold and the value of inventory.

If the amount of inventory increased during an accounting period, the amount of period costs charged to expense during the period would be less than under a direct costing system since some portion of the costs would be applied to inventory. Alternatively, if the amount of inventory on hand declined during the period, the costs that had previously been applied to this inventory would also decline, thereby forcing it to be expensed in the current period. This means that costs would be higher than under the direct costing system. Only if the level of inventory remained perfectly stable from period to period (an unlikely occurrence) would the costs charged to expense in each period be the same, irrespective of the costing method used.

Given these differences, there are a few reasons why a company might want to use direct costing for internal reporting of the valuation of inventory. One is to guard against fraud. This problem arises when a company has a history of, or wishes to avoid, situations where plant managers authorize massive overproduction, which greatly increases inventory valuations and reduces the amount of expense charged to the current period, thereby making their production facilities look inordinately profitable. By eliminating the temptation to build inventories through the capitalization of overhead costs, corporate-level managers can determine which production facilities are doing the best job of controlling costs rather than storing them in inventory.

Direct costing can also be used for inventory valuation when the cost accounting staff is so short-handed, or the accounting system so primitive, that it is difficult to compile a reasonably accurate inventory analysis for management that can track how much inventory has been charged to or taken out of the warehouse in each period and exactly what the components of these costs are. This is a problem particularly if there are constant fluctuations in the valuation of inventory from period to period, resulting in wild swings in the reported level of profitability. As a result, managers may opt to entirely avoid applying overhead costs to inventory except at the end of the fiscal year and even then may leave this chore for the external auditors to complete or at least review in detail.

Though these are limited cases in which direct costing can be used for inventory valuation, they are surprisingly common, especially the second case. Many organizations that do not regularly issue financial reports to the public prefer to avoid absorption costing of their inventory until the end of the fiscal year, and then promptly revert back to direct costing at the beginning of the next fiscal year.

CASE STUDY

The Atlanta division of the General Research and Instrumentation Company manufactures a plastic casing for an electronic compass that is assembled at the same facility. A plastic injection molding supplier has visited the plant and made an offer to construct this casing for $1.42 per unit. Would this result in improved profits for the company?

The first step is to determine which costs are relevant to the decision. The cost of the product is listed on the company's accounting records as $2.48, which comprises:

	Cost
Batch setup costs	$0.32
Direct materials	1.20
Machine depreciation	0.09
Machine maintenance	0.20
Machine operator benefits	0.15
Machine operator labor	0.35
Machine utilities	0.04
Material handling labor	0.10
Scrap	0.03
Total	$2.48

Initially the decision appears to be an easy one, for the internal cost is well above the price the supplier is willing to charge. However, before we write the purchase order to the supplier, let us review the data in a different manner by stripping out costs that would disappear at both the unit level and batch level if the casing were no longer produced internally. This analysis reveals:

	Unit Costs	Batch Costs	Other Costs
Batch setup costs		$0.32	
Direct materials	$1.20		
Machine depreciation			$0.09
Machine maintenance			0.20
Machine operator benefits			0.15
Machine operator labor			0.35
Machine utilities			0.04
Material handling labor			0.10
Scrap	0.03		
Total	$1.23	$0.32	$0.93

This further analysis reveals a somewhat different picture of the internal cost of the casing. Now we see that most of the cost elements are overhead costs related to the injection molding machine or its operator, neither of which will be eliminated if the casing is withdrawn from production and given to the supplier. Since these costs will still be present under any scenario, they should not be considered when making the make-or-buy decision. However, we are still left with the remaining two elements of the casing cost, the direct materials and the related scrap, and batch setup costs. It is evident that the material cost varies directly with the number of units produced and so is relevant to the decision. But what of the setup cost? Machine setup in this instance is performed by a highly specialized injection molding technician who supervises the installation of a new mold in the machine and verifies that the correct clamping pressure and temperature are set to produce new products. This person is paid on an hourly basis, and goes home if there is no setup work to do. Under this scenario the setup cost is a direct cost and so is relevant to the decision. If the setup person had been a salaried employee who would be paid irrespective of the presence of the casing work, then this would not have been a relevant cost.

Based on the preceding analysis, we find that both the unit- and batch-level costs of producing the compass casing are direct costs, which total $1.55. Since this cost is higher than the cost charged by the supplier, the company elects to accept the supplier's offer and outsource the production of the compass casing.

This case study demonstrates that many of the costs charged to a product are nothing more than allocations and have no relevance in determining the incremental cost of producing it.

SUMMARY

There are many situations in which a direct costing analysis can be of use to a company. It is most useful in reviewing problems with a short-term time frame for which production volumes fall within the current range of capacity. However, if a company has a large proportion of overhead costs, is considering issues with a longer-term time frame, or is looking for solutions that require significant changes in the level of capacity, the direct costing methodology does not yield accurate results. Nonetheless, when used prudently, direct costing is a valuable tool that should be carefully stored in every cost accountant's tool chest.

4

Standard Costing

This chapter covers an old topic—integrating standard costing into the accounting function. This practice gained popularity early in the twentieth century, both as a means for comparing actual operating results to a standard and as a way to reduce the accounting effort required to process transactions related to the production process. With the advent of ever more powerful computing systems, there is less need to use standard costing as a labor-saving approach to accounting; this view has spawned a movement that has advocated doing away with standard costs entirely, claiming that actual costs should be used for the majority of accounting applications.

In this chapter we consider the various functions in which standard costs can be used, as well as instances where this method is no longer valid. As the reader will see, there are still situations where standard costing can be of considerable benefit, though one must now be more selective in using it than was previously the case.

PURPOSE OF STANDARD COSTS

A standard cost has a number of potential uses. A company can design its standards to apply to just one of these uses or to many, depending on its needs. The main purposes of standard costs are listed here, along with a discussion of the situations in which each use is most applicable:

- ○ **Budgeting.** A standard can be set for any type of cost that is the amount expected to be incurred in each accounting period in the future. It can be a total dollar amount per period or a cost per unit of output that varies in total, depending on the total amount of activity that occurs. It is especially useful when a company builds tables of information relating the incurrence of different costs to specific levels of activity, so that projected changes in activity levels can be related back to precisely defined standard costs. Actual activity can then be compared to these standard costs to determine where a corporation is not doing a good job of controlling costs.

o **Variance analysis.** An adjunct to the budgeting use of standard costs is their use in determining the variances from actual costs incurred and investigating the nature of these costs. Much concern has been expressed in accounting circles that too much time and effort are spent in defining and investigating variances, especially in just-in-time manufacturing environments where rapid information feedback is required.

o **Pricing.** If there is a full set of standard costs on hand, one can quickly determine the projected price of a product rather than laboriously researching actual costs, resulting in an increase in the speed of price quoting.

o **Financial closing.** It is easier to compile costs for inventories and determine the cost of goods sold if standard costs per unit are used rather than actual costs, resulting in a faster closing of the financial books at the end of each accounting period. However, since nearly all companies have converted from manual to computerized accounting systems, this method is much less of an advantage than was previously the case.

o **Cost smoothing.** Standard costing includes the use of predetermined overhead rates, which results in the incurrence of a standard amount of overhead expense in each period that conforms to the level of activity. This practice is in opposition to the immediate expensing of all overhead costs as they are incurred, which tends to result in significant swings in expenses from period to period. When standard overhead costs are used, the amount of overhead expense recognized in any given period is much smoother than it would be otherwise.

However, those favoring direct costing (Chapter 3) feel that this approach hides overhead costs more properly related to the current period and so should not be carried forward to a future period despite the resulting variability in the level of overhead expense recognized.

Thus, there are several reasons for using standard costing. Though concerns have been expressed about some of the purposes noted here, it is a rare company that finds no use at all for the standard costing concept in some of its accounting activities. However, to be sure of one's need for this approach, we next address in more detail the problems that have been encountered with standard costing.

PROBLEMS WITH STANDARD COSTS

The opposition to standard costing has grown more intense over the last few years. Though the problems outlined in this section do not herald the elimination of standard costing, one should keep in mind that some of the points noted here are valid ones; consequently, standard costing must now be selectively implemented only in particular situations rather than automatically installed at every company. Here are the main problem areas to be aware of:

- ○ **Not useful in a continuous improvement environment.** Standard costs, as noted in the next section, are designed to be the expected cost of a product or activity for some period of time into the future. This means that the expected lifetime of a standard cost is generally considered to be at least a full year, and in many cases it is not expected to change at all unless the underlying processes are altered. However, in today's increasingly common environment of continuous improvement, a standard cost may be rendered invalid by the end of the month, thereby requiring the time-consuming formulation of a new standard. Given this rapid degree of change, a case can be made for eliminating standard costs entirely.

- ○ **Not useful for short product lives.** It takes a fair degree of effort and time to compile a standard cost. This is a problem when a product has a short life span, since the standard cost may not even be available until the product has been on the market for a few months and will be useful for only a few more months before the product is rendered obsolete and replaced. This problem occurs particularly in the high-technology arena, where products may last in the market for as little as a month.

○ **Does not result in rapid feedback of cost information.** The traditional cost accounting system accumulates production quantities for an entire month, compiles their standard costs, and feeds this information back to the production staff shortly after the end of the month. This is too slow for many organizations with just-in-time manufacturing systems, for they need to have costing information immediately, before their short production runs are completed. For them, perusing standard cost variances a month after a production run is simply a waste of time.

○ **Does not yield information at the batch level.** Most standard costing systems accumulate costs in total for an accounting period and churn out variances that apply to the entire manufacturing operation. This approach yields no information about problems at the batch production level, which is where most issues arise. The problem can be mitigated to some extent by accumulating costs at a more detailed level.

○ **Results in contrary purchasing behavior.** One of the variances resulting from a standard costing analysis is the price variance, which determines the amount of excess materials cost a company incurred in manufacturing a product. The presence of this variance forces the purchasing staff to focus a large part of its attention on lowering the price of materials. Though this may seem like a rational use of purchasing time, it can be taken too far, so that excess quantities are purchased or inferior components are acquired—all to ensure that there is no unfavorable purchase price variance.

○ **Results in contrary production scheduling behavior.** The labor efficiency variance also results from a standard costing system; it itemizes the cost of excess labor time incurred by an operation. This was a closely watched variance in the days of large batch runs and a large labor component to total costs, for it gave managers an incentive to operate long production runs that were cost-effective on a per-unit basis. However, now that production runs tend to follow just-in-time principles and are of short duration, the presence of this variance gives production schedulers an incentive to schedule long production runs when they are not called for—simply in an effort to improve labor efficiency, though this is no longer a major cost item.

- **Results in contrary labor scheduling behavior.** One of the most common ways to create a positive direct labor variance is to avoid the use of direct labor entirely by bringing in employees who are officially categorized as indirect labor. The workload stays the same, but the accounting system is distorted so that the situation appears to have improved. This practice also tends to be less efficient, since indirect labor personnel may not be as well trained in production methods.

- **Perpetuates inefficiencies.** When a standard cost is compiled, the industrial engineer doing the work determines the standard amount of labor and material inefficiency and scrap currently in the production process, or that expected in the near term, and includes these costs in the standard. Organizations driving toward zero inefficiency find that the use of standard costs distracts their focus because they want their employees to eliminate *all* inefficiency, rather than allowing some inefficiency to be included in the standards.

- **Labor standards are not accurate.** In many instances the accuracy of labor costs is substantially worse than that for material costs because the designer of a standard fails to take into account a number of additional factors, such as downtime, break time, and training. Consequently, the standard cost of labor does not accurately reflect reality.

- **Shifts management focus toward labor variances.** Several of the variances generated by a standard costing system are related to direct labor. Even though the quantity of this cost has gradually declined in many companies, to the point where it is one of the smallest costs included in the production process, the existence of these variances forces managers to investigate adverse variances even if their total dollar amount is relatively minor. This issue can of course be eliminated by not reporting direct labor variances.

One cannot help but notice that the list of problems associated with standard costs mentioned in this section is longer than the list of favorable items described in the last section. Despite this disparity, there are still situations where standard costs are of great use. The main point in favor of standard costing is that it creates a benchmark against which one can compare performance. Even if the standard carries with it the possibility of being inaccurate, it is still a basis of comparison. Also, if the adverse changes in management behavior caused by the existence of direct labor variances is a problem, one can always stop reporting them to management. Further, if the current manufacturing environment is one where continuous improvement practices constantly alter actual costs, it may still be possible to locate some aspects of the production process whose costs vary so little that standards can still be constructed for them. By making these adaptations to the existing production system, one can still selectively find a place for standard costing in most organizations.

FORMULATION OF STANDARD COSTS

A number of factors go into the formulation of standard costs. First, one must determine who creates these standards. The setting of material and labor standards for products is usually the job of the industrial engineering staff, though the cost accountant may assist this department in compiling costs for the standards. A representative from the purchasing department may also be assigned to this work, since the purchasing staff can determine how raw material costs are altered at different volume levels. If standards are being created for overhead costs, the lead designer is usually the cost accountant instead of an industrial engineer since there is no need to include details of the production process in the formulation of overhead standards.

Another issue is the timing of changes in the creation of standards. The decision to update a standard is based on several factors. For example, if a company's costs rarely change (an unusual circumstance), reformulation of a standard can be undertaken perhaps as rarely as once every few years. However, given the rapid rate of cost fluctuation with which most companies now deal, a more common situation is to at least update material cost standards whenever there is a significant change in the underlying actual material costs.

The same applies to labor standards. The labor price component of a labor standard is generally changed whenever there is a bulk alteration in actual labor rates, for example, when a new union contract goes into effect. In between these periods there is no reason to alter this standard at all. However, the labor efficiency portion of a standard may need to be changed more frequently. Whenever a labor-saving device or process is installed, there is a decrease in the amount of labor needed to complete a product, which justifies a change in the standard. Given the frequency of these incremental changes, before making a change in the labor standard, the industrial engineering staff usually waits until several efficiency changes have combined to produce a significant alteration in the amount of required labor. This reduces the work of the engineering staff, while still keeping the labor standards relatively accurate.

Overhead standards are generally adjusted with much less frequency than material or labor standards. Typically, they are altered at the beginning of each fiscal year, when the accounting staff reviews and adjusts overhead rates from the previous year.

An issue that impacts the timing of all types of standards is the amount of effort required to make adjustments. This includes not only the time of the cost accounting and engineering staff, who must analyze standards, but also that of the accounting staff, who must make changes in the accounting records and explain the resulting variances to management. This is a major problem for organizations without a sufficient number of staff. Thus, even if costs change continually, it is quite likely that a company simply does not have the resources to make timely updates to standards.

Another issue that impacts the timing of changes in standard costs is the use of these costs in inventory valuation. Though there is no specific accounting rule stating that standard costs cannot be used for inventory valuation, the standards must be close enough to actual costs that there is essentially no difference between the standard cost of an inventory item and its actual cost. To ensure that this is the case, a company that uses standard cost inventory valuation must make a large number of adjustments to standard costs over the course of a year. In this case accounting rules force one to update standards with greater frequency.

One last situation that impacts the timing of standards adjustment is their use as cost controls. If this is a major purpose of standards, then it is essential that they accurately reflect actual costs rather than be outmoded standards that have not been updated for some time. If a company neglects regular updates, its standard costs will not be useful as a basis for cost control.

Having discussed who creates and adjusts standards, as well as their timing, we next address *how* standards are created. In general, any type of standard is a carefully compiled cost that ignores all past inefficiencies and instead focuses on the short-term future cost of the item in question. In this way one sets a goal that a company can attempt to attain in the short run. Formulation of this standard cost should include a consideration of these factors:

○ **Learning curve.** Labor efficiencies are driven by the level of experience the production staff achieves while creating a specific product. The staff becomes more efficient as the volume of the product manufactured increases. Thus, any projected increase in production volume can be expected to result in added labor efficiencies.

○ **Production volume.** All types of standards—labor, materials, and overhead—are based to some extent on the volume of projected production. For example, increased production volume results in greater purchasing volumes, which drive down the unit price for components purchased.

○ **Substitute materials.** In many instances there is some substitution of materials for those listed in a product's standard bill of materials. This may be a result of periodic material shortages. If the problem arises at regular intervals, it may be necessary to include an average cost of materials in a product's standard cost that is the combined cost of the regular material and its substitute.

○ **Equipment layout.** The efficiency of the workforce is strongly influenced by the layout of equipment in the production facility. If the distances between machines are considerable, additional labor costs will be involved when materials are moved to the next machine in the sequence. This situation can also impact material scrap rates because materials are batched before they are moved the long distance to the next machine; scrap can build up in these batches before anyone discovers it and corrects the problem.

○ **Equipment condition.** An old machine processes materials less efficiently than a new one if only because it requires more frequent adjustment. This impacts the efficiency of the labor force and may increase material scrap rates.

○ **Inventory accuracy.** If the inventory system does not yield accurate inventory tracking information, there are likely to be material shortages from time to time that stop production. This in turn reduces the efficiency of direct labor, which must either wait for new materials to be found or shift to a different machine to perform other work.

○ **Work instructions.** If there are no instructions attached to a job, or if these instructions are difficult to interpret, the direct labor staff may not be able to set up or run a job with the optimal level of efficiency.

○ **Production scheduling system.** The method for scheduling jobs throughout the production facility has a major impact on the amount of production that can be run through a plant. For example, when there is a focus on producing small batches of products rather than on long runs, more time is devoted to setting up and breaking down jobs, which reduces the time available for production.

○ **Speed of equipment setup.** Much of the time required for a production run is taken up by switching the tooling on a machine. A company that constantly works to reduce this setup time can devote more of the total time of a production run to actually producing product, which reduces its cost.

○ **Test runs.** It may not be possible to estimate a standard for a new product without first operating a test run of the production process and estimating production times from this test.

Other alternatives are to use engineering studies or an analysis of past experience, adjusted for future expected conditions.

○ **Anticipated collective bargaining results.** The standard labor price can be reasonably estimated for companies with unions since there is a historical record of the rates that other companies have settled for in the past.

Clearly, there are many factors to consider when creating a standard cost. Though not all the information sources noted here will be used to develop a single standard, a combination of sources will probably be used for the creation of each one. By using multiple sources of information, such as an engineering study or historical records, one can compare and contrast information, which is helpful in finding and eliminating data that is clearly inaccurate or inconsistent.

A final factor to consider when generating a standard cost is the type of standard to be published. Should it be a theoretical standard, one that reflects past results, or perhaps one that is just attainable? Some issues related to each perspective are:

○ **Theoretical standard.** This is a standard cost that can be reached only if the company runs its operations perfectly— machines never break down, the staff is always on hand, there is no scrap, and production volumes are maximized. While it is nice to know what the absolute lowest cost can be, using such a cost as a standard can frustrate the staff since it can never hope to match this standard, much less surpass it. Also, if only the standard costs of products are charged to inventory, all excess costs—which may be considerable with this type of standard—will be charged to the current period, skewing the reported financial results.

○ **Historical standard.** This standard cost is essentially the average of costs actually experienced in the recent past. This type of standard closely reflects near-term costs, especially if there are no significant changes in the workforce or production systems. However, this standard has a great deal of inefficiency built into it, which gives employees no incentive to surpass it by achieving greater efficiency.

○ **Attainable standard.** This standard cost is lower than the historical standard but not as low as the theoretical standard. It incorporates a reasonably achievable level of inefficiency, which roughly corresponds to the expected increases in efficiencies the facility can be expected to attain in the near term. With this standard employees have a reasonable cost goal as their target. Also, if attainable standard costs are used to compile the cost of inventory, the amount charged to inventory will be somewhat lower than in the case of historical standards but higher than for theoretical standards.

Of the various types of standards considered here, the recommended one is the attainable standard, for it represents a cost that the organization will not find hopelessly out of reach (i.e., a theoretical standard) nor will it be too easy to match (i.e., the historical standard). Instead, it is one that can be reached through the implementation of changes that are reasonably achievable.

STANDARD COSTS FOR PRICING

As noted at the beginning of this chapter, price quotes can be compiled much more quickly with standard costs than with actual ones because actual costs can require a great deal of research. For example, if a customer requests a quote on an order size of 20,000 units, the sales department must call for an emergency meeting with the cost accountant to lay out the volume requirements of the quote; the cost accountant must then find some evidence of previous component part purchase volumes in the same range or ask the purchasing staff to research this information for her. Then she must go to the production scheduling department to determine the typical setup time for the production run required to produce the requested product and consult the production manager or industrial engineering staff about the required machine and assembly effort required to create the product. Finally, she must go back to the accounting department to determine what the overhead charge will be. Then she compiles the collected cost estimates and takes them to the sales department—where everyone is wondering why it took so long to provide the quote.

A much simpler approach is to create a set of standard costs that are readily accessible by the sales department and which can be plugged into a standard quoting model that itemizes all the costs of the order. The salesperson answering the customer's request may even be able to keep the customer on the phone, while entering information in the quote model, and return a quote to the customer at once. This method reduces the price quoting time from days to minutes.

There are two key factors to consider when using this type of quoting model. First, any significant changes in actual costs must be updated in the standard costs fed into the quoting model as soon as possible so that quotes are not based on faulty data. This problem is most acute for products with a large proportion of purchased parts, since a modest change in a price charged to the company by a supplier will result in a significant change in profits if the cost change is not immediately passed on to the customer. The second and much larger problem is that the database of standard costs must include standards for different ranges of production volume. For example, the setup cost for any production run is the same, but the cost of the setup is spread over many more units when the run is a large one, thereby reducing the cost per unit. Similarly, the cost of purchased parts drops when they are purchased in large volumes for a large customer order. Also, labor efficiencies increase for a large production run since workers require less time per unit when many units are being produced. Given the impact of volume on standard costs, multiple standard costs for a broad range of potential volumes should be stored in the computer system. Without this information the sales staff is able to issue quotes for only a narrow range of order quantities, reducing much of the efficiency obtained by using standard costs for product pricing.

STANDARD COSTS FOR BUDGETING

The most obvious use of standard costs is in budgeting. A standard cost is used as the basis of comparison for actual costs incurred during an accounting period. This is an excellent use since there must be some standard against which an actual cost can be compared to ensure that incurred costs fall within a range predetermined to be satisfactory.

For budgeting purposes the existing standard cost for products and activities must be updated to reflect expected costs in the period against which the standard cost is matched. For example, if the current rental rate per month is $80,000 but the lease agreement clearly specifies that the rate will increase to $92,000 per month in the budget period, the budgeting standard set for that month must be $92,000. If numerous changes in the standard are expected during the budget period, the budget should reflect these changes. Another way to budget for this situation is to keep the standard amount the same for the entire set of budgeted periods but to add a budgeted variance for periods in which a change from the standard is anticipated.

The use of standard costs in a budget has a unique advantage in that these costs are not incorporated directly into accounting transactions through the use of variances, as can be the case for cost of goods sold or inventory transactions (as described in a later section). Instead, they are keypunched into a separate file containing only budget information. This file is not used in accounting transactions but is simply added to financial reports that compare actual costs to budgeted costs.

STANDARD COSTS FOR INVENTORY

A common use for standard costs is to apply them to a company's inventory. By doing so, one can rapidly determine the cost of inventory just by having a firm grasp on the quantities of inventory on hand rather than the individual actual cost of each item. This approach simplified the work of cost accountants for a number of years, especially before the advent of computer systems, which make it much easier to trace the actual cost of a purchased item. Despite the use of computers, this method is still a valid one, for tracing actual costs through work in process is quite difficult—using standard costs in this area is most helpful in quickly compiling costs that are reasonably accurate. The main issue here is that the speed and efficiency with which the accounting staff can value all portions of an inventory are greatly improved by the use of standard costs.

It may not be necessary to use standard costs for inventory valuation if a company has a small inventory or uses just-in-time systems. In both cases there is so little inventory on hand, or it passes through the facility so quickly, that its value is no longer a significant element of the balance sheet and so requires little attention. However, most companies still have thousands of parts in stock or have complex products that spend a great deal of time moving through the production process. For these organizations standard costs are still the best approach for valuing inventory.

One issue that arises when standard costs are used for inventory valuation is the frequency with which changes should be made in the standards. Changes should be made as often as is necessary to ensure that total actual costs closely approximate total standard costs. This rule is based on the requirement that standard costs can be used for external financial reporting purposes only if they closely match actual costs. Thus, many organizations undertake a comprehensive comparison of standard costs to actual costs as often as once a month. Since this level of frequency invalidates the reason for using standards—they require less work—a better approach is to determine which elements of a standard cost comprise the bulk of the total cost and then track these specific costs with great frequency while other costs are reviewed at greater intervals. For example, a piece of hard candy is made almost entirely of sugar and corn syrup, with all other materials comprising less than 2% of the total cost. Therefore, it is reasonable to adjust the standard cost of this product for just these two components at regular intervals and leave the remaining costs for an annual review.

Another way to save labor when changing standard costs is to cluster components by commodity code for reporting purposes and then review them at the commodity level with different amounts of frequency, depending on which commodities are the most volatile in price.

Once standards are in place, a company will find that variances from the standard that inevitably arise must be charged to the current period's cost of goods sold or stored in inventory. Which is the correct method? From an external financial reporting perspective, actual costs should be used to value inventory, and the actual cost is the standard cost plus (or minus) any related variances. From this point of view, variances should be rolled into the cost of inventory. However, any excess cost over a standard can be considered a wasted cost since the standard cost represents the amount that should be expended during purchasing and production. According to this view, waste should be charged to the current period. The decision of where to put variances is not a small one because charging variances to the current period alters the level of reported profits, which in turn impacts the amount of income taxes paid. The preferred method is to avoid charging variances to inventory. This reasoning involves not just avoiding taxes but also the efficiency of the accounting staff, for charging variances to inventory requires the maintenance of a separate variance inventory account, which must be reconciled in each reporting period. In short, it is easier to charge variances to the cost of goods sold.

The issue of whether to store variances from standards in the inventory can be reduced in scope by using standard costs only for certain stages of inventory. For example, raw materials can be carried on the accounting books at actual cost, while work-in-process costs are charged as standard costs. This is a particularly appealing way to handle the problem, especially if there is already a computer system in place that does an adequate job of tracking the actual cost of goods purchased. The reason for using only standard costs for work-in-process activities is that they involve many activities taking place over a short time frame, which results in a large quantity of cost-related information that must be handled by the cost accounting staff whenever something moves through the production process. By switching to standard costs for just this part of the inventory, a cost accountant can reduce the paperwork needed to determine the actual added cost of work-in-process activities.

Another method is to calculate the cost of all types of inventory using standard costs, but also to determine variances from the standard at all stages of the production process and adjust the inventory balance continuously so that the total cost of inventory recorded on the books is essentially the same as its actual cost. For example, a component is purchased and received, at which point it is recorded at its actual cost. Before the component travels to the shop floor for inclusion in the production process, its standard cost is compared to the actual cost and a variance is immediately recorded. Once the component finishes running through the production process, any additional standard costs are compared to actual costs, and any further variances are disposed of. This may seem like a great deal of work, and it certainly is. However, it has the benefit of providing managers with immediate knowledge of variances and also makes it possible to issue accurate daily financial statements. These benefits are considerable but must be weighed against the substantial cost of conducting daily examinations of variances.

A special case sometimes arises when a standard cost is changed to such a large extent that the incremental difference in standard costs causes a significant change in the recorded value of inventory. For example, a new union contract is approved that increases the labor rate by 10%. When labor standards are increased to reflect this change, the value of the inventory suddenly jumps since much of the inventory contains some element of labor cost whose value has now increased. To offset this problem, one can determine the value of the inventory before making a standard cost change, calculate the difference after the change, and alter the recorded value of the inventory to offset the change caused by the alteration in standards. Since there may be many standard cost changes every month, it is not efficient to complete such an analysis for every change. Instead, the adjustment effort should be reserved for only the largest changes. All other alterations tend to be too small to warrant a special costing adjustment.

One case in which the use of standard costs is *not* acceptable is in the costing of a specific product that will be charged to a customer at a price having a direct relationship to the costs incurred to produce it. For example, the government may offer a company a cost-plus contract to create a customized item. The company must compile its actual costs, add a predetermined margin percentage, and bill this total to the government. There is no standard cost because the product is a unique one that requires the compilation of actual costs. Since actual costs must be tracked, it would be a duplication of labor to create standard costs, too.

In this section we have discussed the situations where standard costs can reduce the labor required to record the valuation of inventory, as well as the (more limited) instances where they do not result in an appreciable reduction in the accountant's work. We have also described the reasoning behind the treatment of variances from standard. One must carefully consider all these factors before deciding whether to use standard costs for inventory valuation and to what extent they should be used.

STANDARD COST ENTRY

How are standard costs incorporated into the accounting system? Thus far we have talked about swapping actual and standard costs into and out of an accounting system as though they are easily substituted car parts—the car runs, no matter which part is installed. In truth the methodology is somewhat different.

Standard costs are compiled in a separate file from all other accounting transactional data. For example, the cost of goods sold is compiled in the accounting system by accumulating the total cost of components purchased during the period, which is stored in the accounts payable file. Labor costs for the period are accumulated from the payroll system, while other overhead costs are drawn from accounts payable records. These are all actual costs and roughly match the amount of cash a company has expended to acquire the resources needed to manufacture its products. Meanwhile, standard costs are accumulated by engineering, purchasing, and cost accounting personnel in an entirely different set of files. At no time are the standard and actual cost files merged.

At the end of the reporting period, the number of units of production is accumulated and multiplied by the standard cost of each unit. The total is then compared to the accumulated actual cost of production (net of any inventory changes). If there is a difference between the two total costs, the total standard cost is assumed to be the correct amount of cost of goods sold; any shortfall or overage in actual costs compared to the standard amount is charged to a variance account. These variances are then broken down into efficiency, price, and volume variances, and further comparisons are then made between the actual costs incurred and the standard cost file.

This approach maintains the "purity" of accounting transactions since actual costs are always recorded for every transaction. It is only when these actual costs are compared to a baseline cost (the standard) that they are split into variances which are recorded in separate accounts.

SUMMARY

In this chapter we saw that there are a number of situations, primarily related to production lines with continuous improvement efforts in place or short product cycles, where actual costs cannot be used effectively. However, cases where it cannot provide some benefit, even if only in a limited form, are quite rare. Many cost accountants find that standard costs are still valuable for product quotes, inventory valuation, budgeting, and variance analysis. They are also beneficial in reducing the labor associated with the analysis and use of actual costs.

5

LIFO, FIFO, and Average Costing

This chapter could also be called "Cost Flow Assumptions" because that is the essence of its content. Cost flows describe the order in which costs are incurred. The reason why cost flows are important is that the cost incurred for an item may change over time, so that different costs appear in the accounting records for the same item. In this situation, how does the cost accountant handle these costs? Are the earliest costs charged off first, or the later ones? Or is there an alternative approach that avoids the issue? In this chapter we look at the last-in first-out (LIFO), first-in first-out (FIFO), and average costing systems and how each one is used under a different assumption of cost flows.

LAST-IN FIRST-OUT METHOD

In a supermarket the shelves are stocked several rows deep with products. Shoppers walk by and pick products from the front row. If the stock clerk is lazy, he will then add products to the front-row locations from which products were just taken rather than shifting the oldest products to the front row and putting the new ones in the back. This concept of always taking the newest products first is called last-in first-out. It is illustrated numerically in Exhibit 5.1, where we list a number of inventory purchases and usages on the first column and note various calculations across the top row.

In the first row of Exhibit 5.1, we purchase 500 units of a product with part number BK0043 on May 3, 20X0 (as noted in the first row of

Exhibit 5.1 LIFO Valuation Example

LIFO Costing: Part Number BK0043

Date Purchased (1)	Quantity Purchased (2)	Cost per Unit ($) (3)	Monthly Usage (4)	Net Inventory Remaining (5)	Cost of 1st Inventory Layer ($) (6)	Cost of 2nd Inventory Layer ($) (7)	Cost of 3rd Inventory Layer ($) (8)	Cost of 4th Inventory Layer ($) (9)	Extended Inventory Cost ($) (10)
05/03/X0	500	10.00	450	50	(50×10.00)				500
06/04/X0	1000	9.58	350	700	(50×10.00)	(650×9.58)			6,727
07/11/X0	250	10.65	400	550	(50×10.00)	(500×9.58)			5,290
08/01/X0	475	10.25	350	675	(50×10.00)	(500×9.58)	(125×10.25)		6,571
08/30/X0	375	10.40	400	650	(50×10.00)	(500×9.58)	(100×10.25)		6,315
09/09/X0	850	9.50	700	800	(50×10.00)	(500×9.58)	(100×10.25)	(150×9.50)	7,740
12/12/X0	700	9.75	900	600	(50×10.00)	(500×9.58)	(50×9.58)		5,769
02/08/X1	650	9.85	800	450	(50×10.00)	(400×9.58)			4,332
05/07/X1	200	10.80	0	650	(50×10.00)	(400×9.58)	(200×10.80)		6,492
09/23/X1	600	9.85	750	500	(50×10.00)	(400×9.58)	(50×9.85)		4,825

data), and use 450 units during that month, leaving 50 units. These 50 units were all purchased at a cost of $2.00 each, so we itemize them in column 6 as our first layer of inventory costs for this product. In the next row of data, we see that an additional 1,000 units were bought on June 4, 20X0, of which only 350 units were used. This leaves an additional 650 units at a purchase price of $9.58, which we place in the second inventory layer, as noted in column 7. In the third row we have a net decrease in the amount of inventory, so this reduction comes out of the second (or last) inventory layer in column 7; the earliest layer, as described in column 6, remains untouched since it was the first layer of costs added and will not be used until all the other inventory has been eliminated. The exhibit continues through seven more transactions, at one point increasing to four layers of inventory costs.

There are several factors to consider before implementing a LIFO system. They are:

○ **Many layers.** The LIFO cost flow approach can result in a large number of inventory layers, as shown in the exhibit. Though this is not important when a computerized accounting system is used that automatically tracks a large number of such layers, it can be burdensome if the cost layers are manually tracked.

○ **Alters the inventory valuation.** If there are significant changes in product costs over time, the earliest inventory layers may contain costs that are wildly different from market conditions in the current period, which could result in the recognition of unusually high or low costs if these cost layers are ever accessed.

○ **Reduces taxes payable in periods of rising costs.** In an inflationary environment costs that are charged to the cost of goods sold as soon as they are incurred result in a higher cost of goods sold and a lower level of profitability, which in turn results in a lower tax liability. This is the principal reason why LIFO is used by most companies.

○ **Requires consistent usage for all reporting.** Under Internal Revenue Service (IRA) rules, if a company uses LIFO to value its inventory for tax reporting purposes, it must do the same for its external financial reports. The result of this rule is that a company cannot report lower earnings for tax purposes and higher earnings for all other purposes by using an alternative inventory valuation method. However, it is still possible to mention what profits would have been if some other method had been used, but only in the form of a footnote appended to the financial statements. If financial reports are generated only for internal management consumption, any valuation method can be used.

○ **Interferes with the implementation of just-in-time systems.** As noted in the last item, clearing out the final cost layers of a LIFO system can result in unusual cost-of-goods-sold figures. If these results cause a significant skewing of reported profitability, company management may be put in the unusual position of opposing the implementation of advanced manufacturing concepts, such as just-in-time, that reduce or eliminate inventory levels (with an attendant highly favorable improvement in the amount of working capital requirements).

In short, LIFO is used primarily for reducing a company's income tax liability. This single focus can cause problems, such as too many cost layers, an excessively low inventory valuation, and a fear of inventory reductions due to the recognition of inventory cost layers that may contain low per-unit costs, which result in high levels of recognized profit and therefore a higher tax liability. Given these issues, one should carefully consider the utility of tax avoidance before implementing a LIFO cost layering system.

FIRST-IN FIRST-OUT METHOD

A computer manufacturer knows that the component parts it purchases are subject to rapid rates of obsolescence, sometimes becoming worthless in a month or two. Accordingly, it is sure to use up the oldest items in stock first rather than running the risk of scrapping them a short way into the future. For this type of environment, the FIFO method is the ideal way to deal with the flow of costs. This method assumes that the oldest parts in stock are always used first, which means that their associated old costs are used first as well.

The concept is best illustrated with an example, which we show in Exhibit 5.2. In the exhibit we list the same data previously used for parts purchases and use in Exhibit 5.1, but now we account for the costs using FIFO instead of LIFO. In the first row we create a single layer of inventory that results in 50 units of inventory at a per-unit cost of $10.00. So far, the extended cost of the inventory is the same as under LIFO, but that changes as we proceed to the second row of data. In this row we have a monthly inventory usage of 350 units, which FIFO assumes will use the entire stock of 50 inventory units left over at the end of the preceding month, as well as 300 units purchased in the current month. This wipes out the first layer of inventory, leaving a single new layer composed of 700 units at a cost of $9.58 per unit. In the third row there are 400 units of usage, which again come from the first inventory layer, shrinking it down to just 300 units. However, since extra stock was purchased in the same period, we now have an extra inventory layer made up of 250 units at a cost of $10.65 per unit. The rest of the exhibit proceeds using the same FIFO layering assumptions.

Several factors must be considered before implementing a FIFO costing system:

○ **Fewer inventory layers.** The FIFO system generally results in fewer layers of inventory costs in the inventory database. For example, the LIFO model in Exhibit 5.1 contained four layers of costing data, whereas the FIFO model in Exhibit 5.2, which used exactly the same data, resulted in no more than two inventory layers. This conclusion generally holds true because a LIFO system leaves some layers of costs completely untouched for long time periods if inventory levels do not drop, whereas a FIFO system continually clears out old layers of costs so that multiple costing layers do not have a chance to accumulate.

○ **Reduces taxes payable in periods of declining costs.** Though it is unusual to see declining inventory costs, this sometimes occurs in industries where there is ferocious price competition among suppliers or high rates of innovation that in turn lead to cost reductions. In such cases, using the earliest costs first results in immediate recognition of the highest possible

Exhibit 5.2 FIFO Valuation Example

FIFO Costing: Part Number BK0043

Date Purchased (1)	Quantity Purchased (2)	Cost per Unit ($) (3)	Monthly Usage (4)	Net Inventory Remaining (5)	Cost of 1st Inventory Layer ($) (6)	Cost of 2nd Inventory Layer ($) (7)	Cost of 3rd Inventory Layer ($) (8)	Extended Inventory Cost ($) (9)
05/03/X0	500	10.00	450	50	(50 × 10.00)			500
06/04/X0	1000	9.58	350	700	(700 × 9.58)			6,706
07/11/X0	250	10.65	400	550	(300 × 9.58)	(250 × 10.65)		5,537
08/01/X0	475	10.25	350	675	(200 × 10.65)	(475 × 10.25)		6,999
08/30/X0	375	10.40	400	650	(275 × 10.40)	(375 × 10.40)		6,760
09/09/X0	850	9.50	700	800	(800 × 9.50)			7,600
12/12/X0	700	9.75	900	600	(600 × 9.75)			5,850
02/08/X1	650	9.85	800	450	(450 × 9.85)			4,433
05/07/X1	200	10.80	0	650	(450 × 9.85)	(200 × 10.80)		6,593
09/23/X1	600	9.85	750	500	(500 × 9.85)			4,925

expense, which reduces the reported profit level and therefore reduces taxes payable.

o **Shows higher profits in periods of rising costs.** Since it charges off the earliest costs first, any recent increase in costs is stored in inventory rather than being immediately recognized. This results in higher levels of reported profits, though the attendant income tax liability is also higher.

o **Less risk of outdated costs in inventory.** Because old costs are used first in a FIFO system, there is no way for old, outdated costs to accumulate in inventory. Thus, the management group does not have to worry about the adverse impact of inventory reductions on reported levels of profit, either with excessively high or excessively low charges to the cost of goods sold. This avoids the dilemma noted earlier for LIFO, where just-in-time systems may not be implemented if the result will be a dramatically different cost of goods sold.

In short, the FIFO cost layering system tends to result in storage of the most recently incurred costs in inventory and higher levels of reported profits. It is most useful for companies whose main concern is reporting high profits rather than reducing income taxes.

AVERAGE COSTING METHOD

The average costing method is calculated exactly in accordance with its name—it involves a weighted average of the costs in inventory. It has the singular advantage of not requiring a database that itemizes the many potential layers of inventory at the different costs at which they were acquired. Instead, the weighted average of all units in stock is determined, at which point *all* the units in stock are accorded this weighted average value. When parts are used from stock, they are all issued at the same weighted average cost. If new units are added to stock, the cost of the additions are added to the weighted average of all existing items in stock, which results in a new, slightly modified weighted average for *all* the parts in inventory (both old and new).

This system has no particular advantage in relation to income taxes since it does not skew the recognition of income based on trends in either increasing or declining costs. This makes it a good choice for organizations that do not want to deal with tax planning. It is also useful for small inventory valuations, where there would not be any significant change in the reported level of income even if the LIFO or FIFO method were used.

Exhibit 5.3 illustrates the weighted average calculation for inventory valuations using a series of 10 purchases of inventory. There is a maximum of one purchase per month, with use (reductions from stock) also occurring in most months. Each of the columns in the exhibit shows how the average cost is calculated after each purchase and use transaction.

We begin the illustration with the first row of calculations, which shows that we have purchased 500 units of item BK0043 on May 3, 20X0. These units cost $10.00 per unit. During the month in which the units were purchased, 450 units were sent to production, leaving 50 units in stock. Since there has been only one purchase, we can easily calculate (column 7) that the total inventory valuation is $500 by multiplying the unit cost of $10.00 (column 3) by the number of units left in stock (column 5). So far, we have a per-unit valuation of $10.00.

Next we proceed to the second row of the exhibit, where we have purchased another 1,000 units of BK0043 on June 4, 20X0. This purchase was less expensive since the purchasing volume was larger, so the per-unit cost for this purchase is only $9.58. Only 350 units are sent to production during the month, so 700 units are now in stock, of which 650 are added from the most recent purchase. To determine the new weighted average cost of the total inventory, we first determine the extended cost of this newest addition to the inventory. As noted in column 7, we arrive at $6,227 by multiplying the value in column 3 by the value in column 6. We then add this amount to the existing total inventory valuation ($6,227 plus $500) to arrive at the new extended inventory cost of $6,727 (column 8). Finally, we divide this new extended cost in column 8 by the total number of units now in stock (column 5) to arrive at our new per-unit cost of $9.61.

The third row reveals an additional inventory purchase of 250 units on July 11, 20X0, but more units are sent to production during that month than are bought, so the total number of units in inventory drops to 550 (column 5). This inventory reduction requires no

Exhibit 5.3 Average Costing Valuation Example

Average Costing: Part Number BK0043

Date Purchased (1)	Quantity Purchased (2)	Cost per Unit ($) (3)	Monthly Usage (4)	Net Inventory Remaining (5)	Net Change in Inventory During Period (6)	Extended Cost of New Inventory Layer (7)	Extended Inventory Cost ($) (8)	Average Inventory Cost/Unit ($) (9)
05/03/X0	500	10.00	450	50	50	500	500	10.00
06/04/X0	1000	9.58	350	700	650	6227	6,727	9.61
07/11/X0	250	10.65	400	550	−150	0	5,286	9.61
08/01/X0	475	10.25	350	675	125	1281	6,567	9.73
08/30/X0	375	10.40	400	650	−25	0	6,324	9.73
09/09/X0	850	9.50	700	800	150	1425	7,749	9.69
12/12/X0	700	9.75	900	600	−200	0	5,811	9.69
02/08/X1	650	9.85	800	450	−150	0	4,359	9.69
05/07/X1	200	10.80	0	650	200	2160	6,519	10.03
09/23/X1	600	9.85	750	500	−150	0	5,014	10.03

review of inventory layers, as was the case for the LIFO and FIFO calculations. Instead, we simply charge off the 150 unit reduction at the average per-unit cost of $9.61. As a result, the ending inventory valuation drops to $5,286, with the same per-unit cost of $9.61. Thus, reductions in inventory quantities under the average costing method require little calculation—just charge off the requisite number of units at the current average cost.

The remaining rows of the exhibit repeat the concepts just noted, alternatively adding units to and deleting them from stock. Though there are a number of columns in this exhibit to be examined, it is really a simple concept to understand and work with. A typical computerized accounting system performs all these calculations automatically.

SUMMARY

An examination of a company's flow of costs will result in the decision to value its inventories based on the LIFO, FIFO, or average costing concept. The LIFO method is the most complex, resulting in reduced profit recognition and a lower income tax liability in periods of rising inventory costs. The FIFO method is almost as complex but tends to result in fewer inventory cost layers; it reports higher profits in periods of rising inventory costs and so has higher attendant tax liabilities. The average costing concept avoids the entire layering issue by creating a rolling average of costs without the use of any cost layers; it tends to provide reported profit figures between those that would be described using the LIFO and the FIFO methods. As more companies reduce their inventory levels with advanced manufacturing techniques such as material requirements planning and just-in-time, they will find that the reduced amount of inventory left on hand makes the choice of a cost flow concept less relevant.

6

Throughput Costing

Every now and then, a completely new idea comes along that can be described as refreshing, disturbing, or both. Within the accounting profession, throughput accounting is that idea. It originated in the 1980s in the writings of Eliyahu Goldratt, an Israeli physicist. It is based on the concept that a company must determine its overriding goal and then create a system that clearly defines the main capacity constraint that allows it to maximize that goal. The changes this causes in an accounting system are startling.

THROUGHPUT DEFINITIONS

A few new terms are used in throughput costing, so we define them before delving into the throughput model. They are:

○ **Throughput.** This is the contribution margin left after a product's price is reduced by the amount of its totally variable costs (explained in the next item). There is no attempt to allocate overhead costs to a product nor to assign any semivariable costs to it. As a result, the amount of throughput for most products tends to be high.

○ **Totally variable costs.** This cost is incurred only if a product is created. In many instances this means that only direct materials are considered a totally variable cost. Direct labor is not totally variable unless employees are paid only if a product is produced. The same rule applies to all other costs, so there are no overhead costs in the "totally variable cost" category.

○ **Capacity constraint.** This is a very important concept in throughput accounting. It is a resource within a company that limits its total output. For example, it may be a machine that can produce only a specified amount of a key component in a given time period, thereby keeping overall sales from expanding beyond the maximum capacity of that machine. It may be the sales staff, which is not large enough to bring in all possible customer orders. It may even be a raw material of which there is not enough to ensure that all orders can be filled. There may be more than one capacity constraint in a company, but rarely more than one for a specific product or product line.

○ **Operating expenses.** This is the sum total of all company expenses, excluding totally variable expenses. Of particular note is that throughput accounting does not care if a cost is semivariable, fixed, or allocated—all costs that are not totally variable are lumped together for the calculation model shown in the next section. This group of expenses is considered the price a company pays to ensure that it maintains its current level of capacity.

○ **Investment.** This definition is the same as the one found under standard accounting rules. However, there is a particular emphasis on a company's investment in working capital (especially inventory), as we will see shortly.

We now use these definitions to create the throughput accounting model in the next section.

THROUGHPUT MODEL

The primary focus of throughput costing is on how to force the most throughput dollars as possible through the capacity constraint, pure and simple. It does this by first determining the throughput dollars per minute of every production job scheduled to run through the capacity constraint and rearranging the order of production priority so that the products with the highest throughput dollars per minute are produced first. The system is based on the supposition that only a certain amount of production can be squeezed through a bottleneck operation, so the production that yields the highest margin must come first in order of manufacturing priority to ensure that profits are maximized. The concept is most easily demonstrated in the example shown in Exhibit 6.1.

In the example there are four types of products a company can sell. Each requires some machining time on the company's capacity constraint, which is the circuit board manufacturing process (CBMP). The first item is a 19-inch color television, which requires 10 minutes of the CBMP's time. The television sells for $150.00 and has associated direct materials of $68.90, which gives it a throughput of $81.10. We then divide the throughput of $81.10 by the 10 minutes of processing time per unit on the capacity constraint to arrive at the throughput dollars per minute of $8.11 shown in the second column of Exhibit 6.1. We then calculate the throughput per minute for the other three products and sort them in high-low order based on which ones contribute the most throughput per minute. This leaves the 19-inch television at the top of the list. Next we multiply the unit demand for each item by the time required to move it through the capacity constraint point. We do not care about the total production time for each item, only the time required to push it through the bottleneck. Then we determine the total amount of time during which the capacity constraint can be operated, which in the example is 62,200 minutes and is noted at the top of the example. We then fill in the total number of minutes required to produce each product in the fifth column, which also shows that we do not have enough time available at the capacity constraint to complete the available work for the high-definition television, which has the lowest priority. Then, by multiplying the throughput per minute by the number of minutes for each product and multiplying the result by the total number of units produced, we arrive at the total throughput for the entire production process for the period, $405,360. However, we are not finished yet. We must still subtract from the total throughput the sum of all the operating expenses for the facility. After they are subtracted from the total throughput, we have achieved a profit of 7.5% and a return on investment of 6.1%. This is the basic throughput accounting model.

So far, this looks like an ordinary analysis of how much money a company can earn from the production of a specific set of products.

Exhibit 6.1 Throughput Model

			Maximum Constraint Time: **62,200**		
Product	Throughput ($/min of constraint)	Required Constraint Usage (min)	Unit Demand/ Actual Production	Cumulative Constraint Utilization	Cumulative Throughput/ Product ($)
19-in. color TV	8.11	10	1,000/1,000	10,000	81,100
100-W stereo	7.50	8	2,800/2,800	22,400	168,000
5-in. LCD TV	6.21	12	500/500	6,000	37,260
50-in. high-definition TV	5.00	14	3,800/1,700	23,800	119,000
			Throughput total		$405,360
			Operating expense total		$375,000
			Profit		$30,360
			Profit percentage		7.5%
			Investment		$500,000
			Return on investment		6.1%

Source: Adapted from T. Corbett, *Throughput Accounting* (Great Barrington, MA: North River Press, 1998), p. 44.

However, there is more here than is at first apparent. The issue is best explained with another example. Let us say that the cost accounting manager arrives on the scene, does a thorough costing analysis of all four products in the preceding exhibit, and determines that, after all overhead costs are properly allocated, the high-definition television actually has the highest gross margin and the 19-inch television has the least. The relative positions of the other two products do not change. The cost accounting manager's summary of the product costs appears in Exhibit 6.2.

According to the cost accounting scenario, we should actually be producing as many high-definition television sets as possible. To test this theory we duplicate the throughput analysis shown earlier in Exhibit 6.1, but this time we move the high-definition television to the top of the list and produce all 3,800 units that are on order, while dropping the 19-inch television to the bottom of the list and producing only as many units as are possible after all other production has been completed. All the other variables stay the same. This analysis is shown in Exhibit 6.3.

According to this analysis, which is based on best cost allocation principles, where we have carefully used activity-based costing to ensure that overhead is closely matched to actual activities, we have altered the mix of products and realized a net *reduction* in profits of $53,360! How can this be possible?

This outcome can be traced to three major problems with the traditional cost accounting method, all of which are corrected through the use of throughput accounting. All three factors con-

Exhibit 6.2 Fully Absorbed Product Costs

Product Description	Price ($)	Totally Variable Cost ($)	Overhead Allocation ($)	Gross Margin ($)
19-in. color TV	150.00	68.90	49.20	31.90
100-W stereo	125.50	65.50	18.00	38.00
5-in. LCD TV	180.00	105.48	41.52	33.00
50-in. high-definition TV	900.00	830.00	20.00	50.00

Exhibit 6.3 Throughput Analysis Using Priorities Based on Overhead Costs

			Maximum Constraint Time: **62,200**		
Product	Throughput ($/min of constraint)	Required Constraint Usage (min)	Unit Demand/ Actual Production	Cumulative Constraint Utilization	Cumulative Throughput/ Product ($)
50-in. high-definition TV	5.00	14	3,800/3,800	53,200	266,000
100-W stereo	7.50	8	2,800/1,125	9,000	67,500
5-in. LCD TV	6.21	12	500/0	0	0
19-in. color TV	8.11	10	1,000/0	0	0
			Throughput total		$333,500
			Operating expense total		$375,000
			Profit		–$41,500
			Profit percentage		–12.4%
			Investment		$500,000
			Return on investment		–8.3%

tributed to the problem just noted in Exhibit 6.3. The first is that we cannot really allocate overhead costs to products and expect to use the resulting information in any meaningful way for incremental decisions of any kind. To do so would be to make the erroneous assumption that overhead costs vary directly with every unit of a product produced or sold. In reality the only cost that varies directly with a product is the cost of its direct material. That is all. Even direct labor is no longer so direct. In how many companies does the staff go home immediately after the last product is completed? Instead, the staff is employed on various projects during downtime periods so that experienced employees are available for work the next day. There is an even less tenuous linkage between machine costs and products. Does a company immediately sell a machine if there is one less unit of production running through it? Of course not. The machine sits on the factory floor and accumulates depreciation and preventive maintenance costs until some other job comes along that requires its services. In short, nearly all the costs of any company can be lumped into a general category called "operating expenses" or something similar. These are simply the costs that a company incurs to maintain a given level of capacity rather than a disaggregated group of costs that are closely tied to specific products. The reason why this concept has such a large bearing on Exhibit 6.3 is that the high-definition television was assumed to have a much higher margin than the 19-inch television on the basis of allocated costs. However, for the purposes of the production runs used in the throughput example, the overhead cost pools assigned to these two products still become valid expenses, whether or not either of the products is produced at all. Consequently, it is detrimental to use overhead as a factor in determining product throughput, no matter what traditional cost accounting principles state.

The second major problem with traditional cost accounting is that it completely ignores the concept of limited production capacity. Instead, the primary goal of a costing analysis is to determine which products have the highest gross margins and which have the least. This information is then used to pursue two goals—selling oodles of the high-margin products while dumping or improving the margins on the low-margin products. Unfortunately, the real world knows that production capacity is limited, so one must choose among the best customer orders available at the moment, only some of which can be run through the capacity constraint and possibly none of which are the highest-margin products the company is capable of producing. Therefore, a simple categorization of which products are "best" or "worst" has no meaning on a day-to-day basis. The real world forces one to choose among possible product sales, which requires one to continually reevaluate a mix of product orders for different products and quantities in relation to each other. In Exhibit 6.3 ignoring the capacity constraint would have led to the much higher profit of $177,360 (assuming that all production is completed for all four products), but of course this was rendered impossible by the capacity constraint.

The final problem, and the one that is clearly the largest inherent flaw in traditional cost accounting, is that it ignores the fact that a company is one large, interactive system and instead strives to achieve lots of local improvements in efficiency. The flaw revealed in the example in Exhibit 6.3 is that the cost accounting manager determined the fully absorbed cost of each product on its own, not realizing that to a significant degree each product shares in the use of many overhead costs. Any type of allocation system results in locally optimized profitability levels for individual products but does not address the fact that the overhead cost pool really services the capacity of the company as a whole, not an individual product. For example, the cost of a production scheduler's salary may be allocated to a product based on the amount of scheduling time required to insert it in the production schedule. But does this added cost really "belong" to the product? If the product were not produced at all, the scheduler would still be there, earning a salary, so it is evident that for the purposes of the throughput model, there is no point in assigning such overhead costs to products. This means that because so many costs are not assignable to products, it is valid to charge totally variable costs only to a specific product; all other costs must be paid for by the combined throughput of *all* the products produced since the overhead applies to all of them. In short, we cannot look at the individual profitability levels of products but rather at how the throughput of all possible product sales, when combined, can be used to offset the total pool of overhead costs.

What we have just seen is that traditional cost accounting methods make multiple mistakes: first, of applying overhead to products for incremental decision-making purposes; second, of ignoring the role of capacity constraints; and finally, of not considering the entire set of products and related operating expenses a complete system for which various combinations of products must be considered in order to determine the highest possible level of profitability. However, we are still dealing with throughput accounting at an abstract level. We now work through a few examples to clarify the concepts presented thus far.

THROUGHPUT ACCOUNTING AND VOLUME PURCHASING DECISIONS

The sales manager of the electronics company in our previous example runs into corporate headquarters flush from a meeting with the company's largest account, Electro-Geek Stores (EGS). He has just agreed to a deal that drops the price of the 100-watt stereo system by 20% but that guarantees a doubling of the quantity of EGS orders for this product for the upcoming year. The sales manager points out that the company may have to hold off on a few of the smaller-volume production runs of other products, but no problem—the company is bound to earn more money on the extra volume. To test this assumption the cost accountant pulls up the throughput model on his computer, shifts the stereo to the top of the priority list, adjusts the throughput to reflect the lower price, and obtains the results shown in Exhibit 6.4.

To be brief, the sales manager has just skewered the company. By dropping the price of the stereo by 20%, much of the product's throughput was eliminated and so much of the capacity constraint was used up that there was little room for the production of any other products that might generate enough added throughput to save the company. This example clearly shows that one must carefully consider the impact on the capacity constraint when debating whether to accept a high-volume sales deal. This is a particularly dangerous area in which to ignore throughput accounting, for the acceptance of a really large-volume deal can hog all the time of the capacity constraint, eliminating any chance for the company to

Exhibit 6.4 Throughput Model with Volume Discounts

Product	Throughput ($/min of constraint)	Required Constraint Usage (min)	Unit Demand/Actual Production	Cumulative Constraint Utilization	Cumulative Throughput/Product ($)
			Maximum Constraint Time: **62,200**		
100-W stereo	4.36	8	5,600/5,600	44,800	195,328
19-in. color TV	8.11	10	1,000/1,000	10,000	81,100
5-in. LCD TV	6.21	12	500/500	6,000	37,260
50-in. high-definition TV	5.00	14	3,800/100	1,400	7,000
					$333,500
			Throughput total		$320,688
			Operating expense total		$375,000
			Profit		−$54,312
			Profit percentage		−16.9%
			Investment		$500,000
			Return on investment		−10.9%

manufacture other products and thereby eradicating any chance of offering a wide product mix to the general marketplace.

THROUGHPUT ACCOUNTING AND CAPITAL BUDGETING DECISIONS

The production and cost accounting managers have been reviewing a number of workstations in the production area and find that they can speed up the production capacity of the circuit board insertion machine, which is the next workstation in line *after* the capacity constraint operation. The speed of this machine can be doubled if the company is willing to invest an extra $28,500. To see if this is a good idea, we once again look at the throughput model. In this instance the only number we change is the investment amount. The results are shown in Exhibit 6.5.

By making the extra investment, the only change in the company's situation is that its return on investment drops by fourth-tenths of a percent. The reason is that any investment used to improve any operation besides the capacity constraint is a waste of money. *The only thing that a company achieves by making such an investment is that it improves the efficiency of an operation that is still controlled by the speed of the capacity constraint.* In reality the situation is even worse, for any newly upgraded subsidiary operation now has greater efficiency and can therefore produce in even greater quantities—all of which turns into work in process that piles up somewhere in front of the bottleneck operation, which increases the company's work-in-process investment. Thus, an investment in a nonbottleneck operation may actually worsen the overall financial results of the company because the investment in inventory increases.

This is an important concept for investment analysis, for the typical cost accountant is trained to examine each investment proposal strictly on its own merits, with no consideration of how the investment fits into the entire production system. If the impact of the capacity constraint were also factored into investment analyses, few of them would ever be approved because they do not have a positive impact on the capacity constraint.

To look at this problem from a different angle, let us say that the company's engineering staff has determined that it can increase the

Exhibit 6.5 Throughput Model and Investment Analysis

Product	Throughput ($/min of constraint)	Required Constraint Use (min)	Unit Demand/ Actual Production	Cumulative Constraint Utilization	Cumulative Throughput/ Product ($)
		Maximum Constraint Time: **62,200**			
19-in. color TV	8.11	10	1,000/1,000	10,000	81,100
100-W stereo	7.50	8	2,800/2,800	22,400	168,000
5-in. LCD TV	6.21	12	500/500	6,000	37,260
50-in. high-definition TV	5.00	14	3,800/1,700	23,800	119,000
			Throughput total		$405,360
			Operating expense total		$375,000
			Profit		$30,360
			Profit percentage		7.5%
			Investment		$528,500
			Return on investment		5.7%

89

speed of the capacity constraint from 62,200 available minutes per month to 70,000 minutes, but only if additional processing work is completed by the machining operation just before the constraint operation, which will cost $51,000 in operating expenses and reduce the available capacity of the preceding operation by 28%. As Exhibit 6.6 shows, this is a good idea, for much of the remaining production that we were unable to schedule can now be processed, creating an added profit of nearly $39,000; the added use of a nonconstraint operation makes no difference since it simply improves the rate of throughput at the capacity constraint. However, a traditional cost accounting analysis might have rejected this proposal because the cost of the additional machining time at the preceding workstation would have been added to the cost of any products running through it, which would have increased their fully burdened price, thereby making their margins supposedly too low to bother with.

These two examples clearly show that examining the cost of an *individual* investment is not sufficient. Instead, we must look at the impact of each new investment on the capacity constraint to see if it changes the throughput level of the system as a whole.

THROUGHPUT ACCOUNTING
AND OUTSOURCING DECISIONS

One of the company's key suppliers has offered to take over the entire production of the 5-inch LCD television, package it in the company's boxes, and drop-ship the completed goods directly to the company's customers. The catch is that the company's cost will increase from its current fully burdened rate of $147.00 (as noted in Exhibit 6.2) to $165.00, which leaves a profit of only $15.00. A traditional cost accounting review would predict that the company will experience reduced profits of $18.00 if this outsourcing deal is completed (the difference between the current and prospective costs of $147.00 and $165.00). To see if this is a good deal, we turn once again to the throughput model, which is reproduced in Exhibit 6.7. In this exhibit we have removed the number from the Cumulative Constraint Utilization column for the LCD television since it can now be produced without the use of the capacity constraint. However, we are still able to put a cumulative throughput dollar figure in the final column for

Exhibit 6.6 Throughput Model with Increased Constraint Time

		Maximum Constraint Time: **70,000**			
Product	Throughput ($/min of constraint)	Required Constraint Usage (min)	Unit Demand/ Actual Production	Cumulative Constraint Utilization	Cumulative Throughput/ Product ($)
19-in. color TV	8.11	10	1,000/1,000	10,000	81,100
100-W stereo	7.50	8	2,800/2,800	22,400	168,000
5-in. LCD TV	6.21	12	500/500	6,000	37,260
50-in. high-definition TV	5.00	14	3,800/2,257	31,600	157,990
			Throughput total		$444,350
			Operating expense total		$375,000
			Profit		$69,350
			Profit percentage		15.6%
			Investment		$500,000
			Return on investment		13.9%

Exhibit 6.7 Throughput Model with an Outsourcing Option

Product	Throughput ($/min of constraint)	Required Constraint Use (min)	Unit Demand/ Actual Production	Cumulative Constraint Utilization	Cumulative Throughput/ Product ($)
			Maximum Constraint Time: **62,200**		
19-in. color TV	8.11	10	1,000/1,000	10,000	81,100
100-W stereo	7.50	8	2,800/2,800	22,400	168,000
5-in. LCD TV	6.21	12	500/500	N/A	7,500
50-in. high-definition TV	5.00	14	3,800/2,129	29,806	149,030
			Throughput total		$405,630
			Operating expense total		$375,000
			Profit		$30,630
			Profit percentage		7.5%
			Investment		$500,000
			Return on investment		6.1%

this product since there is some margin to be made by outsourcing it through the supplier. By removing the LCD television's use of the capacity constraint, the company is now able to produce more of the next product in line, which is the high-definition television. This additional production allows it to increase the amount of throughput dollars, thereby creating $270.00 more profits than was the case before the outsourcing deal.

Once again, the traditional cost accounting approach would have stated that profits would be lowered by accepting an outsourcing deal that clearly costs more than the product's internal cost. However, by using this deal to release some capacity at the bottleneck, the company is able to earn more money on the production of other products.

THROUGHPUT ACCOUNTING
AND UNPROFITABLE PRODUCTS

The company has just completed a lengthy activity-based costing analysis that has altered the allocation of overhead costs. It is now apparent that much more overhead must be charged to the high-definition television than was previously thought to be the case. This results in a clear loss for the product. Accordingly, the cost accounting manager writes a memo to the management team outlining his reasons for requesting that this product be immediately pulled from the company's production. To see what effect this will have on company profits, we return to the throughput model, as noted in Exhibit 6.8, and remove the line item for the high-definition television.

The model reveals that dropping only this product *reduces* the company's ability to create throughput that can be used to cover the existing pool of operating expenses, thereby creating a loss. This issue highlights a classic problem with traditional cost accounting—allocating overhead to a product does not mean that eliminating the product also eliminates the associated overhead. To ensure that overhead costs are really eliminated, one must carefully review each overhead line item and verify that it can indeed be dropped, as well as create a plan to ensure that actions are taken to eliminate it. Otherwise, the cost will be retained but there will be less throughput available to pay for it.

Exhibit 6.8 Throughput Model without an Unprofitable Product

Product	Throughput ($/min of constraint)	Required Constraint Use (min)	Unit Demand/ Actual Production	Cumulative Constraint Utilization	Cumulative Throughput/ Product($)
			Maximum Constraint Time: **62,200**		
19-in. color TV	8.11	10	1,000/1,000	10,000	81,100
100-W stereo	7.50	8	2,800/2,800	22,400	168,000
5-in. LCD TV	6.21	12	500/500	6,000	37,260
			Throughput total		$286,360
			Operating expense total		$375,000
			Profit		-$88,640
			Profit percentage		-30.9%
			Investment		$500,000
			Return on investment		-17.7%

To take this issue to its logical extreme, the same pool of overhead costs are now allocated to the remaining (and smaller) set of products, which drives up their costs once again. Based on this new information, yet another product is dropped because of a lack of profits, which results in even larger losses and another iteration of cost increases. By focusing instead on the level of throughput that each product generates, one can avoid this overhead allocation trap.

THROUGHPUT AND TRADITIONAL ACCOUNTING COMPARED

In the last few sections we have addressed examples of how throughput accounting yields results different from those reached using more traditional cost accounting methods. In this section we cover additional differences in several other areas.

One of the most popular accounting methodologies is activity-based costing (ABC), which is covered in detail in Chapter 8. Though the author enthuses in that chapter about how ABC can be used to determine the exact causes of overhead (which can be used to tightly control costs), there is another side to this activity. The problem is that ABC reviews require an inordinate amount of time on the part of a number of employees to examine detailed costing information about every facet of a company's operations. Throughput accounting avoids all this work and instead focuses its attention on what it will take to force as much production volume as possible through the capacity constraint, which will increase profits. This laser beam focus requires much less analysis effort than for ABC, which yields more time for the accounting staff to complete other work.

Along similar lines, the management team (as well as the accountants) finds that its efforts are widely spread out over any number of projects when they rely on ABC information, since these analyses focus on the optimization of *all* resources rather than just the capacity constraint. This leaves less time to work on bottleneck-related issues. Throughput accounting, however, ignores problems in other parts of a facility in favor of a detailed analysis of only the capacity constraint, which tends to focus management's attention on improving throughput in this one area.

Another difference between traditional and throughput accounting is that most accountants are trained to report on overhead and direct costs, which in turn draws the attention of managers to tightly controlling these costs. Though this is still a concern in the throughput accounting arena, its primary focus is on increasing the flow of production through the bottleneck operation. Thus, the first method draws attention to reducing costs, while the other attempts to increase revenues.

Yet another difference is that a throughput accountant is interested in the ability of the organization to exactly meet the production schedule for all components that feed into the bottleneck operation, as well as the schedule for the bottleneck itself. Any interruption in this schedule has a direct and immediate impact on revenues. Thus, the throughput accountant delves into the reasons why these schedules are not met—missing materials, improper manning, machine downtime, and so on. None of these activities is a common pursuit of the traditional accountant, who is concerned only with the cost of activities and products.

Another significant difference is that a system that focuses on throughput requires a considerable amount of excess capacity at the work centers that feed the capacity constraint. The reason for this excess is that any shortage in production at a feeder operation reduces the amount of materials flowing to the bottleneck operation, which in turn impacts the amount of production that can flow through it. Accordingly, it is quite acceptable, if not mandatory, to have excess capacity in these feeder operations. When dealing with throughput capacity issues, one should divide the total amount of capacity at each work center into three parts. The first is productive capacity, which is the portion of the total work center capacity needed to process currently scheduled or anticipated production. The second is protective capacity, which is the additional portion of capacity that must be held in reserve to ensure that a sufficient quantity of parts can be manufactured to adequately feed the bottleneck operation. Any remaining capacity is called idle capacity. Only the last type can be eliminated from feeder work centers. The concept of protective capacity is completely foreign to traditional accounting theory, which holds that *all* excess capacity should be eliminated.

Another difference is that traditional cost accounting methodology clearly states that pricing should include fully absorbed costs plus an acceptable profit margin. The sales and marketing staff chafes under this formulation, since it is sometimes confronted with offers from customers to buy large quantities of product at reduced prices, but the accountants will not approve the lower prices. However, throughput theory holds that *any* price point that exceeds the totally variable cost of a product should be considered. To say the least, this offers the sales staff a much larger degree of flexibility! Now projected prices can be included in the throughput model presented several times earlier in this chapter in order to see whether the prices will increase the total throughput of the organization. If not, the proposed price will not be offered to customers. However, if it improves the mix, new price points may be acceptable. Also, the sales staff does not need to deal with a complex absorption costing formula for each product it needs to price. Instead, all it needs is the totally variable cost and the throughput model. The level of simplicity and ease of understanding make the throughput model the preferable device for pricing.

Another pricing issue treated differently in the traditional and throughput systems is the pricing of customer orders that involve small batch sizes. Under the ABC model the cost of setups is assigned to a product's cost, which can be an overwhelmingly large cost if the batch is sufficiently small. Not so under throughput accounting, which holds that the people doing the setups are employed (and paid) by the company even if they are not performing any setups— therefore the setup cost is a fixed cost that should not be assigned to a specific product. Given this assumption (a large one in some instances), the sales staff can still sell small batches to customers at prices not far above their totally variable costs. This tends to result in a company offering a much richer mix of order sizes and products to its customers, which can result in greater market share. However, this concept must be used with caution, for ignoring the cost of setups leads to larger operating expenses in the long run, as many more staff are hired to manage the larger number of production jobs and setups.

Since we are discussing the topic of setups and job lot sizes, this is yet another difference. Traditional accounting holds that one should run long jobs so that the cost of setting up each job can be spread over more units of production. Throughput accounting holds a mixed view of the situation. On one hand, it prefers long production runs at the capacity constraint since this results in more throughput. On the other hand, all feeder work centers should have short runs since this tends to reduce the amount of lead time required to switch over to the production of parts that can be used immediately in the bottleneck operation.

A further difference is that traditional cost accounting focuses on determining a product's gross margin at the most common, or standard, price and recommending that this product be produced if the standard margin is positive. Throughput accounting prefers to review the throughput of each product at every possible price point. For example, if a product is selling to one customer for $10.00 and to another one for $9.50, there is a difference in throughput of $0.50, meaning that the second customer order is ranked lower in the throughput model of scheduled production than the first one and may not be produced at all if there are other products with better throughputs. Thus, it is crucial to examine the price point of *every* customer order.

Another issue is that throughput accounting places greater emphasis on scheduling work through the capacity constraint that can be sold immediately rather than parked in inventory. The reason is that sending products to inventory results in a drop in profits, which cannot be earned until the product is sold and shipped to a customer. Using the bottleneck to increase the size of the inventory is a waste of available capacity. Since the more traditional cost accounting methodology does not recognize the existence of capacity constraints in a system, it does not point out this problem to management.

An interesting difference is in the treatment of quality-related issues. Accountants have greatly increased their focus on the cost of quality over the last few decades, having realized that the cost of repairing products and customer relations damaged by quality issues is extremely expensive. A common result is the preparation of a lengthy cost-of-quality report that itemizes problem areas in every part of a company. Management then prioritizes these problems and works to reduce the overall cost of quality. As one might expect by now, the throughput approach cares only about the impact of quality on the capacity constraint. When a quality problem results in the bottleneck operation not being fed a sufficient quantity of materials or subcomponents, the company's total throughput drops, resulting in a loss of profits. Therefore, quality reporting under this scenario requires one to focus solely on work centers that feed the capacity constraint.

This issue rolls into a related one, the costing of scrap. Under traditional cost accounting the cost of any scrapped item is its fully absorbed cost. Under throughput accounting it is its totally variable cost—if the point at which the item is scrapped is prior to the capacity constraint. If after it, the cost of the scrap rises substantially. The reason for the increase is that the scrapped item must now be replaced with another one that will use up time being processed through the bottleneck operation. Thus, the cost of scrap that occurs after the bottleneck is really its totally variable cost plus the lost throughput that would have been realized if the item had been sold. This is a unique concept—the cost of scrap depends on where it occurs in the production process!

A final difference is the strategic placement of the capacity constraint. The bottleneck operation can be one that is not planned, but a wise management team carefully determines exactly where it should be and plans accordingly. The most typical location is at the most expensive work center. By placing it there managers can keep investment in new machinery at a minimum. Alternatively, a traditional costing system does not even know where the bottleneck operation is located. As a result, excess funds may be invested in increasing the capacity of a bottleneck operation, which may not result in a sufficient increase in throughput to justify the increased investment.

There are obviously a great many differences between traditional and throughput accounting. Clearly, it is very important to view a number of costing-related decisions in terms of the throughput accounting model to ensure that one's decisions do not change from this viewpoint. Next we review the problems with throughput accounting. The following information can be of use when determining the usefulness of information generated by this model.

PROBLEMS WITH THE THROUGHPUT MODEL

The chief problem with the active use of throughput accounting for short-range alterations in the mix of production is that it can *really* annoy customers. When throughput accounting is the driving force behind all production scheduling, a customer who has already placed an order for a product that will result in a suboptimal profit level for the manufacturer may find that its order is never filled. The order continues to fall to the bottom of the manufacturer's list of open orders until the mix of existing orders creates an opening at the capacity constraint that allows it to be produced. Theoretically, this means that some customers may never receive their orders. This issue can be resolved through the use of scheduling policies that require customer orders to be produced, no matter what profitability level will result, after a certain time period has elapsed.

A related problem is that a company's ability to create the highest level of profitability is now dependent on the production scheduling staff who decides what products are to be manufactured and in what order. Because this group has never been involved with profitability issues, there may be some confusion in the scheduling department in terms of how the daily production schedule is to be completed. Should the overriding priority be on throughput? Or must consideration also be given to how long some customers have waited for their orders to be completed? Or should the schedulers still rely on suggested scheduling criteria that can be extracted from the manufacturing resources planning system in the computer? Given the number of issues that must now be dealt with by the schedulers, the best approach may be to have daily schedule review sessions attended by all interested parties, in order to arrive at a production schedule generally agreeable to everyone.

Another issue is that all costs are totally variable in the long run since management then has time to adjust them to long-range production volumes. This being the case, the totally variable cost element of the throughput formula really should include far more than just direct materials if it is used for long-range planning. Otherwise, the management group will operate under the misconception that the entire block of operating expenses is fixed and immovable.

The problems noted here are relatively minor ones and can certainly be overcome with the correct supporting procedures. When balanced against the considerable benefits of this approach, it is apparent that throughput accounting is a major new tool for the cost accountant.

REPORTING WITH THE THROUGHPUT MODEL

When the throughput model is used for financial reporting purposes, the format appears slightly different. The income statement includes only direct materials in the cost of goods sold, which results in a "throughput contribution" instead of a gross margin. All other costs are lumped into an "operating expenses" category below the throughput contribution margin, yielding a net income figure at the bottom. All other financial reports stay the same. Though this single change appears relatively minor, it has one significant impact.

The primary change is that throughput accounting does not charge any operating expenses to inventory, so that they can be expensed in a future period. Instead, all operating expenses are realized during the current period. As a result, any incentive for managers to overproduce is completely eliminated because they cannot use the excess amount to shift expenses out of the current period, thereby making their financial results look better than they would otherwise.

Though this is a desirable result, such a report can be used only for internal reporting purposes because of the requirement of generally accepted accounting principles that some overhead costs be charged to excess production. Nonetheless, it may be worthwhile to use this format internally if it is used to rate the performance of managers.

SYSTEMIC CHANGES REQUIRED FOR ACCEPTANCE OF THE THROUGHPUT MODEL

Unfortunately, throughput accounting requires an entirely different view of the world, one that does not have a logical linkage with the more traditional forms of cost accounting. This will make it difficult for it to gain acceptance.

The main problem is that this method does not use cost as the basis for the most optimal production decisions; instead it uses throughput. This is entirely contrary to the teachings of any other type of accounting, which hold that the highest-margin products (with varying degrees of direct and overhead costs attached to them) should always be produced first. Given that the underpinnings of

traditional cost accounting are threatened by throughput accounting, we come to an all-or-nothing decision—one uses either throughput or traditional costing exclusively. Or is there a way to merge the
two? Here are some thoughts on the subject:

- ○ **Inventory valuation.** Generally accepted accounting principles clearly state that the cost of overhead must be appor-
  tioned to inventory. Throughput accounting states that none
  of the overhead cost should be so assigned. In this case, since
  the rules are so clear, it is apparent that throughput accounting loses. The existing accounting system must continue to assign costs, irrespective of how throughput principles are used
  for other decision-making activities.

- ○ **Inventory investment analysis.** Here there are fundamental
  differences between the two methodologies. Both hold that
  the objective is to always keep one's investment at a minimum. In the case of traditional cost accounting, this is because the return on investment is higher when the total dollar amount of the investment is forced to the lowest
  possible level. Throughput accounting, however, wants to
  shrink the amount of investment because it includes work-
  in-process inventory in this category; it tries to keep WIP
  levels down so that waste is reduced in the production system. In short, the first system advocates a small investment
  for financial reasons, while the latter system favors it because it makes more operational sense. Despite the differences in reasoning, the same conclusion is reached by both
  methodologies. However, the throughput approach is still
  better, for it forces one to analyze all inventory reduction
  projects in light of how they together will impact the capacity constraint, rather than individually.

- ○ **Capital investment analysis.** Because traditional cost accounting only analyzes each investment proposal on its own, rather
  than considering its impact on the production process as a
  whole, it tends to recommend investments that will result in an
  incremental investment but no overall change in the level of
  corporate capacity, which is driven by capacity constraint.

Throughput accounting, however, has a tight focus on investments only in areas that impact the capacity constraint—all other investment proposals are rejected. In this instance it is best to reject the traditional system and conduct analyses based on throughput principles.

○ **Product costing.** Under throughput accounting a product has only a totally variable cost, which may be far lower than the fully absorbed cost that would be assigned to it under more traditional costing systems. This totally variable cost is almost always direct materials, which is an easily calculated figure. Full-absorption costing, however, requires a large amount of calculation effort before a detailed cost can be compiled for a product. Given the wide range in costing outcomes, there is a significant issue in terms of which one to use. For companies selling to the government under cost-plus contracts, there are lengthy, detailed requirements for what variable and overhead costs should be assigned to each product manufactured. These rules virtually require the use of absorption costing—throughput costing is not a viable option. For companies that do not require detailed costing justifications when selling their products, it may be possible to use the much simpler throughput accounting approach.

○ **Production scheduling.** Existing production scheduling systems do not include any kind of throughput modeling that tells production planners which orders should be produced first. It may be possible to customize existing systems or to upgrade packaged software so that this option is available to planners. This would allow them to produce the items that result in the highest throughput per minute of the capacity constraint. However, despite the impassioned arguments of most advocates of throughput accounting, the author does not think that this "improvement" is useful. Any company that has already received a customer order has an obligation to fill it, even if the resulting sale will reduce its overall level of profit from the theoretical maximum that can be calculated with throughput accounting. Maximizing short-term profits by ignoring orders is tantamount to long-term suicide since customers will leave in droves. Consequently, production planners should be left alone to schedule production in the traditional manner, rather than basing their decisions on short-term profit maximization.

○ **Long-term planning.** This is a prime usage area for throughput accounting. One can estimate the approximate sales levels for each product type over a long time frame, such as a year (as well as the price point at which each one will sell), enter it into the throughput model, and determine what mix of prospective sales will result in the highest level of profitability. This method is much superior to the use of throughput costing for short-term production decisions since long-term planning sidesteps problems by avoiding existing customer orders that will result in low profits. Long-term planning does not involve existing customer orders (since they have not been placed yet), so that decisions to produce various types of products at different price points can be made before the sales force goes out to obtain orders.

○ **Price setting.** The sales and marketing staff favors throughput accounting because the margin on products is simple to obtain—just subtract totally variable costs from the price. This beats the often incomprehensible jargon and maze of allocations accompanying activity-based costing systems. Price setting in the throughput environment focuses more on what products can be inserted into the existing production mix at a price that will incrementally increase overall profits, rather than the painful accumulation and allocation of costs to specific products. Throughput is the clear choice here, based on ease of understandability and the speed with which information can be accumulated.

Existing corporate systems are not designed to work with throughput accounting because it uses such a startlingly different approach to determine what products to sell. There are some special cases where it cannot be used at all, such as for inventory valuation and cost-plus billings to customers. However, there are several optimal cases where throughput can bring immediate discernible value to a company. These areas are product pricing, long-term planning, and investment analysis.

SUMMARY

Throughput accounting is a fresh, unique view of how to handle decision making within a company. It has a multidecade battle on its hands to gain acceptance simply because it runs counter to so much established practice in the cost accounting field, an area that will be completely overthrown if throughput ever gains general acceptance. Whether or not other people take to it, the reader should give this approach a great deal of thought, find situations where it can be applied, work it into existing decision-making models, and use it during presentations to management. This method will result in different types of production and sales decisions that will lead to higher levels of profitability; if other people choose not to use it, the reader will have a competitive advantage over them until they choose to do so.

7

Joint and By-Product Costing

In many instances companies operate a single production process that results in several products, none of which can be clearly identified through the early stages of production. Examples of such merged production occur in the wood products industry, where a tree can be cut into a wide variety of end products, and in the meatpacking industry, where an animal carcass can be cut into a number of different finished goods. Up to the point in the production process where individual products become clearly identifiable, there is no clear-cut way to assign costs to products. We consider several cost allocation methods in this chapter that deal with this problem and also discuss the usefulness (or lack thereof) of these allocation methods.

NATURE OF JOINT COSTS

To understand joint products and by-products, one must have a firm understanding of the split-off point. This is the last point in a production process where it is impossible to determine the nature of the final products. All costs that have been incurred by the production process up until this point—both direct and overhead—must somehow be allocated to the products that result from the split-off point. Any costs incurred thereafter can be charged to specific products in the normal manner. Thus, a product that comes out of such a process has allocated costs from before the split-off point and costs that can be directly traced to it that occur after the split-off point.

A related term is "by-product," which refers to an additional product that arises from a production process but whose potential sales value is much smaller than that of the principal joint products obtained from the same process. As we will see, the accounting for by-products can be somewhat different.

A complication of the joint cost concept is that there can be more than one split-off point. Exhibit 7.1 diagrams meat processing in a slaughterhouse, where the viscera are removed early in the process, creating a by-product. This is the first split-off point. Then the ribs are split away from the carcass at a second split-off point. The ribs may in turn be packaged and sold at once, or processed further to produce additional products such as prepackaged barbequed ribs. In this instance some costs incurred through the first split-off point may be assigned to the by-product viscera (to be discussed later), while costs incurred between the first and second split-off points are no longer assigned to the viscera but must in turn be assigned to the remaining products that can be extracted from the carcass. Finally, costs that must be incurred to convert ribs into final products are assigned directly to these products. This is the basic cost flow for joint products and by-products.

REASONING BEHIND JOINT AND BY-PRODUCT COSTING

As we will see in the next section, the allocation of costs to products at the split-off point is essentially arbitrary in nature. Though two

Exhibit 7.1 Multiple Split-off Points for Joint Products and By-Products

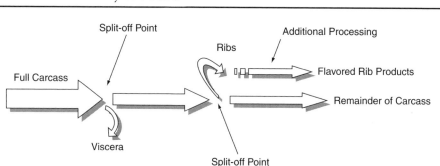

standard methods are used, neither leads to information that is useful for management decision making. Why, then, must the cost accountant be concerned with the proper cost allocation method for joint products and by-products?

Because there are accounting and legal reasons for doing so. Generally accepted accounting principles require that costs be assigned to products for inventory valuation purposes. Though the costs incurred by a production process up to the split-off point cannot be clearly assigned to a single product, it is still necessary to find some reasonable allocation method for doing so in order to obey the accounting rules. Otherwise, all costs incurred up to the split-off point could reasonably be charged directly to the cost of goods sold as an overhead cost, which would result in enormous overhead costs and few direct costs (only those incurred after the split-off point).

The logic for allocating costs to joint products and by-products has less to do with a scientifically derived allocation method and more with finding a quick, easy way to allocate costs that is reasonably defensible (as we will see in the next section). The reason for using simple methodologies is that the promulgators of GAAP realize that there is no real management use for allocated joint costs—they cannot be used to determine break-even points, setting optimal prices, or figuring out the exact profitability of individual products. Instead, they are used for any of the purposes listed here, which are more administrative in nature:

- **Bonus calculations.** Manager bonuses may depend on the level of reported profits for specific products, which in turn is partly based on the level of joint costs allocated to them. Thus, managers have a keen interest in the calculations used to assign costs, especially if some of the joint costs can be dumped onto products that are the responsibility of a different manager.

- **Cost-plus contract calculations.** Many government contracts are based on reimbursement of a company's costs, plus some predetermined margin. In this situation it is in a company's best interests to ensure that the largest possible proportion of joint costs is assigned to jobs that will be reimbursed by the customer; the customer is equally interested, but because of a desire to *reduce* the allocation of joint costs.

○ **Income reporting.** Many organizations split their income statements into sublevels that report on profits by product line or even individual product. In such cases joint costs may make up such a large proportion of total production costs that these income statements do not include the majority of production costs unless they are allocated to specific products or product lines.

○ **Insurance reimbursement.** If a company suffers damage to a production or inventory area, some finished goods or work-in-process inventory may be damaged or destroyed. Then it is in the interests of the company to fully allocate as many joint costs as possible to the damaged or destroyed stock so that it can receive the largest possible reimbursement from its insurance provider.

○ **Inventory valuation.** It is possible to manipulate inventory levels (and therefore the reported level of income) by shifting joint cost allocations toward products stored in inventory. This practice is obviously discouraged since it results in changes to income that have no relationship to operating conditions. Nonetheless, one should be on the lookout for the deliberate use of allocation methods that alter the valuation of inventory.

○ **Transfer pricing.** A company can alter the prices at which it sells products among its various divisions so that high prices are charged to the divisions located in high-tax areas, resulting in lower reported levels of income against which these high tax rates can be applied. A canny cost accounting staff chooses the joint cost allocation technique that results in the highest joint costs being assigned to products being sent to such locations (and the reverse for low-tax regions).

Next we look at the two most commonly used methods for allocating joint costs to products, which are based on product revenues for one method and gross margins for the other.

JOINT COST ALLOCATION METHODS

Though several joint cost allocation methods have been proposed in the accounting literature, only two have gained widespread acceptance. The first is based on the sales value of all joint products at the split-off point. To calculate this value the cost accountant compiles all costs accumulated in the production process up to the split-off point, determines the eventual sales value of all products created at the split-off point, and assigns these costs to the products based on their relative values. If by-products are associated with the joint production process, they are considered too insignificant to be worthy of any cost assignment, though revenues gained from their sale can be charged against the cost of goods sold for the joint products. This is the simplest joint cost allocation method and is particularly attractive because the cost accountant needs no knowledge of any production processing steps that occur after the split-off point.

This different treatment of the costs and revenues associated with by-products can lead to profitability anomalies at the product level. The difficulty is that the determination of whether a product is a by-product or not can be quite judgmental; in one company, if a joint product's revenues are less than 10% of the total revenues earned, it is a by-product, while another company might use a 1% cutoff figure instead. Because of this vagueness in accounting terminology, one company may assign all its costs only to joint products with an inordinate share of total revenues and record the value of all other products as zero. If a large quantity of these by-products is held in stock at a value of zero, the total inventory valuation will be lower than another company would calculate, simply because of its definition of what constitutes a by-product.

A second problem with the treatment of by-products under this cost allocation scenario is that they can be sold only in batches, which may occur only once every few months. This can cause sudden drops in the cost of joint products in the months when these sales occur since these revenues are subtracted from their cost. Alternatively, joint product costs appear to be too high in periods when there are no by-product sales. Thus, one can alter product costs through the timing of by-product sales.

A third problem related to by-products is that the revenues realized from their sale can vary considerably based on market demand. In such cases these altered revenues cause abrupt changes in the cost of the joint products against which these revenues are netted. It certainly may require some explaining by the cost accountant to show why changes in the price of an unrelated product caused a change in the cost of a joint product! This can be a hard concept for a nonaccountant to understand.

The best way to avoid the three issues just mentioned is to avoid designating *any* product a by-product. Instead, each joint product should be assigned some proportion of total costs incurred up to the split-off point, based on its total potential revenues (however small they may be), and no resulting revenues should be used to offset other product costs. By avoiding the segregation of joint products into different product categories, we can avoid a variety of costing anomalies.

The second allocation method is based on the estimated final gross margin of each joint product produced. The calculation of gross margin is based on the revenue that each product will earn at the end of the entire production process, less the cost of all processing costs incurred from the split-off point to the point of sale. This is a more complicated approach because it requires the cost accountant to accumulate additional costs through the end of the production process, which in turn requires a reasonable knowledge of how the production process works and where costs are incurred. Though it is a more difficult method to calculate, its use may be mandatory in instances where the final sale price of one or more joint products cannot be determined at the split-off point (as is required for the first allocation method), thereby rendering the other allocation method useless.

The main problem with allocating joint costs based on the estimated final gross margin is that final gross margin can be difficult to calculate if there is a great deal of *customized* work left between the split-off point and the point of sale. Then it is impossible to determine in advance the exact costs that will be incurred during the remainder of the production process. In such a case the only alternative is to make estimates of expected costs that will be incurred, base the gross margin calculations on this information, and accept the fact that the resulting joint cost allocations may not be provable based on the actual costs incurred.

The two allocation methods described here are easier to understand with an example, which is shown in Exhibit 7.2. In the exhibit we see that $250.00 in joint costs has been incurred up to the split-off point. The first allocation method, based on the eventual sale price of the resulting joint products, is shown beneath the split-off point. In it the sale price of the by-product is ignored, leaving a revenue split of 59%/41% between products A and B. The joint costs of the process are allocated between the two products based on this percentage. The second allocation method, based on the eventual gross margins earned by each of the products, is shown to the right of the split-off point. This calculation includes the gross margin on the sale of product C, which was categorized as a by-product and therefore ignored in the preceding calculation. This calculation results in a substantially different sharing of joint costs among the various products than we saw for the first allocation method, with the split now being 39%/58%/3% among products A, B, and C, respectively. The wide swing in allocated amounts between the two methods can be attributed to the different bases of allocation—the first is based on revenue, whereas the second is based on gross margins.

PRICING OF JOINT PRODUCTS AND BY-PRODUCTS

The key operational activity in which joint cost allocations should be ignored is the pricing of joint products and by-products. The issue here is that the allocation used to assign a cost to a particular product does not really have any bearing on the actual cost incurred in creating the product—either method for splitting costs among multiple products, as noted in the last section, cannot really be proven to allocate the correct cost to any product. Instead, we must realize that all costs incurred up to the split-off point are sunk costs that will be incurred no matter what combination of products is created and sold from the split-off point forward.

Because everything prior to the split-off point is considered a sunk cost, pricing decisions are concerned only with the costs incurred *after* the split-off point because these costs can be directly traced to individual products. In other words, incremental changes in prices should be based on the incremental increases in costs that accrue to a product after the split-off point. This can result in inordi-

Exhibit 7.2 Joint Cost Allocation Methods Example

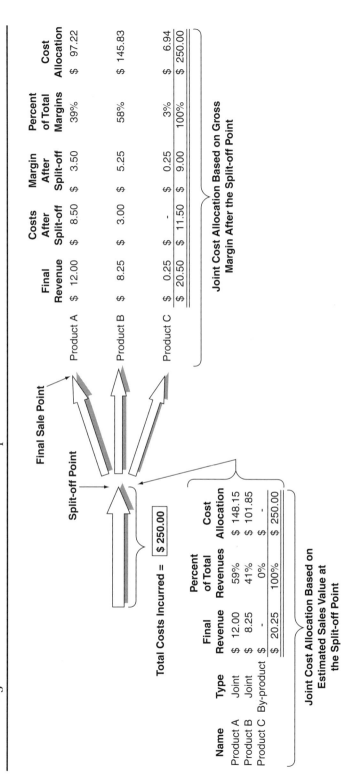

	Final Revenue	Costs After Split-off	Margin After Split-off	Percent of Total Margins	Cost Allocation
Product A	$ 12.00	$ 8.50	$ 3.50	39%	$ 97.22
Product B	$ 8.25	$ 3.00	$ 5.25	58%	$ 145.83
Product C	$ 0.25	$ -	$ 0.25	3%	$ 6.94
	$ 20.50	$ 11.50	$ 9.00	100%	$ 250.00

Joint Cost Allocation Based on Gross Margin After the Split-off Point

Final Sale Point

Split-off Point

Total Costs Incurred = $ 250.00

Name	Type	Final Revenue	Percent of Total Revenues	Cost Allocation
Product A	Joint	$ 12.00	59%	$ 148.15
Product B	Joint	$ 8.25	41%	$ 101.85
Product C	By-product	$ -	0%	$ -
		$ 20.25	100%	$ 250.00

Joint Cost Allocation Based on Estimated Sales Value at the Split-off Point nately low costs being assigned to products because so few costs are incurred after the split-off point. This can occur in response to competitive pressures or because it seems necessary to add only a modest markup percentage to the incremental costs incurred after the split-off point. If these prices are too low, the revenues resulting from the entire production process may not be sufficiently high for the company to earn a profit.

The best way to ensure that pricing is sufficient for a company to earn a profit is to create a pricing model for each product line. Such a model, as shown in Exhibit 7.3, itemizes the types of products and their likely selling points, as well as the variable costs that can be assigned to them subsequent to the split-off point. Thus far, the exhibit results in a total gross margin earned from all joint and by-product sales. Then we add up the grand total of all sunk costs incurred prior to the split-off point and subtract this amount from the total gross margin. If the resulting profit is too small, the person setting prices will realize that individual product prices must be altered in order to improve the profitability of the entire cluster of products. Also, by bringing together all the sales volumes and price points related to a single production process, one can easily see where pricing must be

Exhibit 7.3 Pricing Model for Joint and By-Product Pricing

Product Name	Price/ Unit ($)	Incremental Cost/Unit ($)	Throughput/ Unit ($)	Number of Sales Units	Total Throughput ($)
Viscera	0.40	0.10	0.30	1	0.30
Barbequed ribs	3.00	1.80	1.20	4	4.80
Flank steak	5.50	1.05	4.35	2	8.70
Quarter steak	4.25	1.25	3.00	4	12.00
Pituitary gland	1.00	0.48	0.52	1	0.52
			Total throughput		$26.32
			Total sunk costs		$30.00
			Net profit (loss)		−$3.68

adjusted in order to obtain the desired level of profits. In the example we must somehow increase the total profit by $3.68 in order to avoid a loss. A quick perusal of the exhibit shows us that two of the products—viscera and pituitary gland—do not generate a sufficient amount of throughput to cover this loss. Accordingly, the sales staff should concentrate the bulk of its attention on repricing the other three listed products in order to eliminate the operating loss.

This format can be easily adapted for use for entire reporting periods or production runs rather than for a single unit of production (as was the case in the last exhibit). Then we simply multiply the number of units of joint products or by-products per unit by the total number of units to be manufactured during the period and enter the totals in the far right column of the same format used in Exhibit 7.3. The advantage of this more comprehensive approach is that a production scheduler can determine which products should be included in a production run (assuming that more than one product is available) to generate the largest possible throughput. For a more comprehensive discussion of throughput costing and how it can be used to generate higher profit levels, the reader should refer to Chapter 6.

SUMMARY

The main point of interest in this chapter is that the allocation of costs through any method discussed here is essentially arbitrary in nature—it results in some sort of cost being assigned to a joint product or by-product, but these costs are useful only for financial or tax reporting purposes, not for management decisions. For the latter issues one should use direct costing from the split-off point onward as the only relevant costs and consider all preceding costs sunk costs.

8

Activity-Based Costing

The cost structure of most organizations contains a small proportion of variable costs, as well as many other costs that are lumped together as overhead. The proportion of overhead to variable costs has gradually increased over the years, until there are now companies with three or more times the amount of their variable costs invested in overhead.

Overhead is an amorphous entity that is difficult to assign to any specific product, customer, product line, project, or activity. For this reason it is difficult for a company to allocate its overhead costs to anything. By default, overhead has been allocated based on the amount of direct labor incurred. This practice occasionally results in an allocation of overhead costs that accurately reflects actual overhead use, but most of the time the allocation is either too high or low, yielding incorrect costs that are useless for any kind of decision making.

Activity-based costing (ABC) was invented in order to introduce a logical system of overhead allocation that would result in better information and improved related management decisions.

SHORTCOMINGS OF TRADITIONAL COST ALLOCATION SYSTEMS

Activity-based costing was developed because of the shortcomings of traditional cost allocation systems. The chief problem with these systems is that they do not allocate overhead in a manner that truly reflects the use of overhead. This is because all overhead costs are lumped into one large overhead cost pool and because of the use of inappropriate allocation measures to spread the cost of this pool to products. The end result is incorrect product costing, which can lead to incorrect decisions based on these costs.

The problem is particularly obvious when the overhead cost pool greatly exceeds the size of the allocation measure, which is frequently direct labor. In some industries where considerable machinery or engineering staff are involved (i.e., the automotive, drug, and aerospace industries), the ratio of overhead to the allocation measure is frequently in the range of 300% to 400%. This means that a slight change in direct labor results in the application of an inordinate additional amount of overhead to a product, which in all likelihood is never justified by changes in its use pattern.

Another problem is that the overhead cost pool is allocated based on only one allocation measure. Many of the costs in the overhead cost pool do not have the slightest relationship to the allocation measure and should not be allocated based on it. Here are some of the costs stored in the overhead cost pool that have no relationship whatsoever to the most common allocation measure, direct labor:

- ○ **Building rent.** A better allocation is based on the square footage of the facility used by the machinery and inventory storage areas related to a product line.
- ○ **Building insurance.** A better allocation is square footage.
- ○ **Industrial engineering salaries.** A better allocation is the total number of units expected to be produced over the lifetime of a product line.
- ○ **Machinery depreciation.** A better allocation is the hours of machine time used.
- ○ **Machinery insurance.** A better allocation is the hours of machine time used.
- ○ **Maintenance costs.** A better allocation is the hours of machine time used.
- ○ **Production scheduling salaries.** A better allocation is the number of jobs scheduled during the accounting period.

○ **Purchasing salaries.** A better allocation is the number of parts in a product or the number of suppliers from whom parts must be purchased.

○ **Utilities.** A better allocation is based on the hours of machine time used.

○ **Warehouse salaries.** There are several better allocations, such as the number of receipts or shipments related to a product or the number of parts it has.

It is evident from the above list that most overhead costs lack the slightest relationship to direct labor and that a good cost allocation cannot depend on just one basis of allocation—several are needed to realistically portray the actual use of each element of overhead.

Another issue is that traditional cost allocation systems tend to portray products made with high levels of automation as being deceptively low in overhead cost. For example, when a high-technology company decides to introduce more automation into one of its production lines, it replaces direct labor with machine hours by adding robots. This shrinks the allocation base, which is direct labor, while increasing the size of the overhead cost pool, which now includes the depreciation, utilities, and maintenance costs associated with the robots. When the overhead cost allocation is performed, a *smaller* amount of overhead is charged to the now-automated production line because the overhead costs are being charged based on direct labor use, which has declined. This makes the products running through the automated line look less expensive than they really are. Furthermore, the increased overhead cost pool is charged to other production lines with large amounts of direct labor, even though these product lines do not have the slightest association with the new overhead costs. The end result is a significant skewing of reported costs that makes products manufactured with automation look less expensive than they really are and those produced with manual labor look more expensive.

Traditional cost allocation systems also tend to portray low-volume products as having the highest profits. This problem arises because the overhead costs associated with batch setups and teardowns, which can be a significant proportion of total overhead costs, are allocated indiscriminately to products with both large and small production volumes; none of the special batch costs associated with a specific short production run is allocated to it. This results in the undercosting of products with short production runs and the overcosting of products with long production runs. This problem is one of the most common in cost accounting and leads to faulty management decisions to increase sales of short-run jobs and reduce sales of long-run jobs, which results in reduced profits as company resources are concentrated on the lowest-profit products.

Based on these examples, it is clear that there are serious problems with the traditional cost allocation system. It does not apportion overhead costs correctly, resulting in management receiving information about products that is correct only by accident and leads to decisions not based on factual data. Activity-based costing was developed in order to correct these shortcomings.

OVERVIEW OF ACTIVITY-BASED COSTING

Before describing an ABC system implementation, it is best to see how the system works, from a determination of project scope to a detailed costing of cost objects. This section presents a lengthy overview of the entire ABC system. For a numerical example illustrating how these concepts are converted to an ABC system, the reader should refer to the case study at the end of this chapter.

An ABC system begins with a determination of the scope of the project. This is a critical step, for creating an ABC system that encompasses every aspect of every department of all corporate subsidiaries takes an inordinate amount of time and resources and may never show valuable results for several years, if ever. We first determine the range of activities that the ABC system is to encompass and the results desired from the system. It is not usually necessary to create an ABC system for simple processes for which the costs can be readily separated and reported on. Instead, activities deserving of inclusion in an ABC system are those that involve numerous machines, complex processes, automation, many machine setups, or a diverse product line. These are areas in which it is difficult to clearly and indisputably assign costs to products or other cost objects. When creating a system scope to include these areas, it may be best to start with just a few of them on a pilot project basis so that the installation team and the affected employees can get used to the new system. The scope can later be expanded to include other areas of sufficient complexity to warrant the use of this system.

Scope considerations should also be expanded to include the level of detailed information the system should produce. For example, an ABC system designed to produce information only for strategic analysis is considered satisfactory if it issues high-level information. This system requires a much lower level of detailed information handling and calculation than one used for tactical-level costing of products, activities, or customers. Thus, the level of detailed information analysis built into the project's scope depends entirely on how the resulting information is to be used.

Another scope issue is the extent to which the ABC system is to be integrated into the existing accounting system. If the project is to be handled on a periodic recalculation basis, rather than being automatically updated whenever new information is introduced into the accounting system, all linkages can be no more than a manual retyping of existing information into a separate ABC system. However, a fully integrated ABC system requires extensive coding of software interfaces between the two systems, which is both time-consuming and expensive. These changes may include some alteration of the corporate chart of accounts, the cost center structure, and the cost and revenue distributions used by the accounts payable and billing functions. These are major changes, so the level of system integration should be a large part of any discussion regarding scope.

A final scope issue is a determination of how many costs from nonproduction areas should be included in the system. For companies with proportionately large production departments, this may not be an issue; but for service companies or those with large development departments, such costs can be a sizable proportion of total costs and should be included in the ABC system. These costs can come from areas as diverse as the research and development, product design, marketing, distribution, computer services, janitorial, and administration functions. Adding each new functional area increases the administrative cost of the ABC system, so a key issue in scope determination is whether the cost of each functional area is large enough to have an impact on the activity costs calculated by the system. Those with a negligible impact should be excluded.

Once we have determined the scope, we next separate all direct materials and labor costs and set them to one side. These costs are adequately identified by most existing accounting systems already, so it is usually a simple matter to locate and segregate the general ledger accounts in which they are stored. The remaining costs in the general ledger should be ones that can be allocated.

Next, using our statement of the scope of the project, we identify the costs in the general ledger that are to be allocated through the ABC system. For example, when the primary concern of the new system is to determine the cost of the sales effort on each product sale, finding the sales and marketing costs is the primary concern. Alternatively, if the purpose of the ABC system is to find the distribution cost per unit, only costs associated with warehousing, shipping, and freight must be located.

With the designated overhead costs in hand, we proceed to store costs in secondary, or resource, cost pools. A secondary cost pool is one that provides services to other company functions without directly supporting any activities that create products or services. Examples of resource costs are administrative salaries, building maintenance, and computer services. The costs stored in these cost pools will later be charged to other cost pools with various activity measures, so the costs should be stored in separate pools that can be allocated with similar allocation measures. For example, computer services costs can be allocated to other cost pools based on the number of personal computers used, so any costs that can reasonably and logically be allocated based on the number of personal computers used should be stored in the same resource cost pool.

In a similar manner we store all remaining overhead costs in a set of primary cost pools. There can be a large number of cost pools for the storage of similar costs, but one should consider that the cost of administering the ABC system (unless it is a rare case of full automation) increases with each cost pool added. Therefore, it is best to keep the number of cost pools under 10. A few standard cost pool descriptions are used in most companies. They are:

○ **Batch-related cost pools.** Many costs, such as purchasing, receiving, production control, shop floor control, tooling, setup labor, supervision, training, material handling, and quality control, are related to the length of production batches.

○ **Product line–related cost pools.** A group of products may
have incurred the same research and development, advertis-
ing, purchasing, and distribution costs. It may be necessary to
split this category into separate cost pools when there are several different distribution channels and the costs of the channels differ dramatically from each other.

○ **Facility-related cost pools.** Some costs cannot be directly allocated to specific products because they relate more closely to
the entire facility. These include building insurance, building
maintenance, and facility depreciation costs.

Other cost pools can be added to these three basic cost pools if the
results will yield a significantly improved level of accuracy or if the extra cost pools will lead to attainment of the goals and scope set at the
beginning of the project. In particular, the batch-related cost pool
can be subdivided into several smaller cost pools depending on the
number of different operations within a facility. For example, a
candy-making plant has a line of cookers, the cost of which can be included in one cost pool, while the cost of its candy extruding machines can be segregated into a separate cost pool, and its cellophane
wrapper machines into yet another. Costs can be allocated quite differently, depending on the type of machine used, so dividing this category into a number of smaller cost pools may make sense. The various sources of product costs are noted in Exhibit 8.1.

Costs cannot always be directly mapped from general ledger accounts into cost pools. Instead, there may be valid reasons for splitting
general ledger costs into different cost pools. An allocation method
that does this is called a resource driver. Examples of resource drivers
are the number of products produced, the number of direct labor
hours, and the number of production orders used. Whatever the type
of resource driver selected, it should provide a logical, defendable
means for redirecting costs from a general ledger account into a cost
pool. There should be a minimal number of resource drivers because
time and effort are required to accumulate each one. In reality, most
companies use management judgment to arrive at a set percentage of
each account to be allocated to cost pools, rather than use a formal
resource driver. For example, the cost of computer depreciation may
be allocated 50% to a secondary cost pool, 40% to a batch-related pri-

Exhibit 8.1 Sources of Product Costs

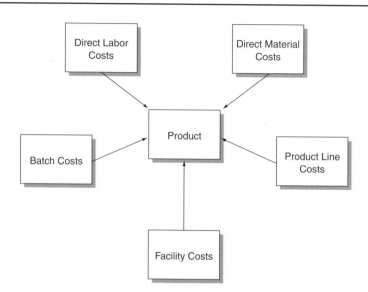

mary cost pool, and 10% to a facility-related primary cost pool because these percentages roughly reflect the number of personal computers located in various parts of the facility. This in turn is considered
a reasonable means of spreading these costs among different cost
pools.

There are varying levels of detailed analysis that one can use to
assign costs to cost pools. The level of analysis is largely driven by the
need for increasingly detailed levels of information; when there is
less need for accuracy, a less expensive method can be used. For example, if there are three cost pools in which purchasing department
salaries can be stored, depending on the actual activities conducted,
the easiest and least accurate approach is to make a management decision to send a certain percentage of the total cost to each one. A
higher level of accuracy requires that the employees be split up into
job categories, with varying percentages being allocated from each
category. Finally, the highest level of accuracy requires time tracking
by employee, with a fresh recalculation after every set of time sheets
is collected. The level of accuracy needed, the size of the costs being
allocated, and the cost of the related data collection drive the decision to collect information at progressively higher levels of accuracy.

The next step is to allocate all the costs stored in secondary cost pools to primary cost pools. This is done with activity drivers, which we will explain shortly. Allocating these cost pools to primary cost pools causes a redistribution of costs that can then be further allocated, with considerable accuracy, from the primary cost pools to cost objects. This subsidiary step of allocating costs from resource cost centers to primary cost centers can be avoided by sending all costs straight from the general ledger to the primary cost pools, but several studies have shown that this more direct approach does not do as good a job of accurately allocating costs. The use of resource cost centers reflects more precisely how costs flow through an organization—from resource activities such as the computer services department to other departments, which in turn are focused on activities used to create cost objects.

Now that all costs have been allocated to primary cost pools, we must find a way to accurately charge these costs to cost objects, which are the users of the costs. Examples of cost objects are products and customers. We perform this allocation with an activity driver, a variable that explains the consumption of costs from a cost pool. There should be a clearly defined cause-and-effect relationship between the cost pool and the activity so that there is a solid, defensible reason for using a specific activity driver. This is important because the use of specific activity drivers changes the amount of costs charged to cost objects, which can raise the ire of the managers responsible for these cost objects. Exhibit 8.2 itemizes a number of activity drivers that relate to specific types of costs.

The list of activities presented in Exhibit 8.2 is by no means comprehensive. Each company has unique processes and costs that may result in the selection of activity drivers different from the ones noted here. There are several key issues to consider when selecting an activity driver. They are:

○ **Minimize data collection.** Few activity drivers are already tracked through the existing accounting system since few of them involve costs. Instead, they are more related to actions, such as the number of supplier reviews or the number of customer orders processed. These are numbers that may not be tracked anywhere in the existing system and so require extra effort to compile. Consequently, if there are few differences

Exhibit 8.2   Activity Drivers for Specific Types of Costs

Cost Type	Related Activity Driver
Accounting costs	Number of billings
	Number of cash receipts
	Number of check payments
	Number of general ledger entries
	Number of reports issued
Administration costs	Hours charged to lawsuits
	Number of stockholder contacts
Engineering costs	Hours charged to design work
	Hours charged to process planning
	Hours charged to tool design
	Number of engineering change orders
Facility costs	Amount of space utilization
Human resources costs	Employee head count
	Number of benefits changes
	Number of insurance claims
	Number of pension changes
	Number of recruiting contacts
	Number of training hours
Manufacturing costs	Number of direct labor hours
	Number of field support visits
	Number of jobs scheduled
	Number of machine hours
	Number of machine setups
	Number of maintenance work orders
	Number of parts in product
	Number of parts in stock
	Number of price negotiations
	Number of purchase orders
	Number of scheduling changes
	Number of shipments
Marketing and sales costs	Number of customer service contacts
	Number of orders processed
	Number of sales contacts made
Quality control costs	Number of inspections
	Number of supplier reviews
Storage time (e.g., depreciation, taxes)	Inventory turnover
Storage transactions (e.g., receiving)	Number of times handled

between several potential activity drivers, pick the one that is already being measured, thereby saving the maintenance work for the ABC system.

○ **Pick low-cost measurements.** If it is apparent that the only reasonable activity measures must be collected from scratch, then—all other factors being equal—pick the one with the lowest data collection cost. This is a particularly important consideration if the ABC project is operating on a tight budget or if employees believe that the new system is consuming too many resources.

○ **Verify a cause-and-effect relationship.** The activity driver must have a direct bearing on the incurrence of costs in the cost pool. To test this relationship, perform a regression analysis; if the regression reveals that changes in the activity driver have a considerable direct impact on the size of the cost pool, it is a good driver to use. It is also useful if the potential activity driver is one that can be used as the basis of measurement for further improvements. For example, if management can focus the attention of the organization on reducing the quantity of the activity driver, a smaller cost pool will result.

Once an activity driver has been selected for each cost pool, we then divide the total volume of each activity for the accounting period into the total amount of costs accumulated in each cost pool to derive a cost per unit of activity. For example, assume that the activity measure is the number of insurance claims processed and that there are 350 in the period. When they are divided into a human resources benefits cost pool of $192,000, the resulting cost per claim processed is $549.

Our next step is to determine the quantity of each activity used by the cost object. To do this, we need a measurement system that accumulates the quantity of activity driver used for each one. This measurement system may not be in existence yet and so must be specially constructed for the ABC system. If the cost of this added data collection is substantial, there will be considerable pressure to reduce the number of activity drivers, which represents a trade-off between accuracy and system cost.

Finally, we have reached our goal, which is to accurately assign overhead costs to cost objects. We multiply the cost per unit of activity by the number of units of each activity used by the cost objects. This should flush out all the costs located in the cost pools and assign them to cost objects in their entirety. Now we have found a defensible way to assign overhead costs in a way that is not only understandable but, more important, can be used by managers to reduce these costs. For example, if the activity measure for the overhead costs associated with the purchasing function's cost is the number of different parts ordered for each product, managers can focus on reducing the activity measure, which entails a reduction in the number of different parts included in each product. Then the amount of purchasing overhead will indeed be reduced, for it is directly associated with and influenced by this activity driver. Thus, the ABC system is an excellent way to focus attention on costs that can be eliminated.

The explanation of ABC has been a lengthy one, so let us briefly recap it. After setting the scope of the ABC system, we allocate costs from the general ledger to secondary and primary cost pools, using resource drivers. We then allocate the costs of the secondary cost pools to the primary cost pools. Next we create activity drivers closely associated with the costs in each of the cost pools and derive a cost per unit of activity. We then accumulate the number of units of each activity used by each cost object (i.e., a product or customer) and multiply this number by the cost per activity driver. This procedure completely allocates all overhead costs to the cost objects in a reasonable, logical manner. An overview of the process is shown in Exhibit 8.3. The case study at the end of this chapter provides a numerical example of this process.

PROBLEMS WITH ACTIVITY-BASED COSTING

Though an ABC system can resolve many difficulties, it has several attendant problems that have resulted in many system installation failures. To ensure a higher degree of success, one should be aware of the problems described in this section and solve as many of them as possible in the earliest stages of an ABC system installation.

Exhibit 8.3 ABC Allocation Process

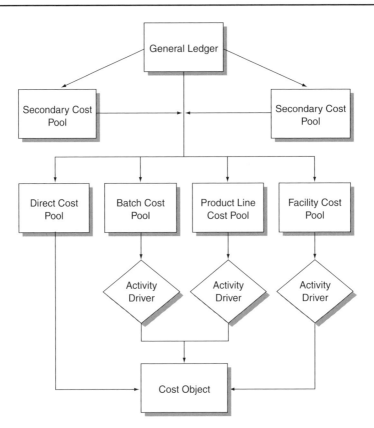

An underlying problem is that company managers hear about the wonders of ABC and demand that it be installed at once—without considering whether their organization actually needs it. ABC is most useful in situations where cost accounting information is muddied by the presence of multiple product lines, machines used to process different products, complex routings, automation, and numerous machine setups. If a company does not meet any of these criteria, it may not need an ABC system. For example, a company with a single product line, one production facility, and a small number of customers can probably generate reasonably accurate costing information from its existing general ledger system without resorting to a lengthy ABC installation. Companies that persist in installing ABC under these circumstances may find that they have achieved only a minor improvement in accuracy at the price of having a second accounting system layered over the existing one.

Another issue is the time required to create an ABC system. This undertaking can be a lengthy one, especially if the desired system is a comprehensive one that straddles multiple product lines and facilities. A project of this magnitude can easily require more than a year to complete. For work of this duration there is a greater chance that opponents of the project will start sniping at it after a few months have passed without any tangible results. In short, the longer the project's duration, the greater the chance that it will be terminated prior to completion. This problem can be avoided by limiting the scope of the ABC project to an area that can be completed, at least as a pilot project, within a much smaller time frame. By taking this approach one can show concrete, valuable results in short order, which builds enthusiasm for a continuing series of ABC projects that will gradually cover the main areas of a company's operations.

A major problem in many instances is that an ABC system extracts information from and reports on the activities of many departments, which draws their ire. If a sufficient number of department managers are irritated by the reports issued by the ABC system, they can use a variety of methods to withhold information from it so that the system no longer yields a sufficient amount of information to make it worthwhile. To avoid this problem, one should ensure that a high-level manager takes personal responsibility for the project so that any interdepartmental problems can be dealt with both quickly and in favor of the ABC system. This also means that great care must be taken to hand off this project sponsor position to succeeding individuals who have an equally high degree of enthusiasm for ABC.

A further issue is that an ABC system almost always involves construction of a set of data separate from the general ledger. If this second database becomes so massive that it is unwieldy, or if the data it contains diverges sharply from the information in the general ledger, the accounting department will offer significant resistance. This conflict arises because staff time must be spent on maintenance—very likely including the hiring of extra cost accounting staff—and the results from the system may be difficult to trace back to the company's financial reports, entailing additional effort by the accounting staff. Thus, an increase in the workload can produce resistance within the

accounting department. To avoid this problem, it is necessary to properly design the ABC system so that it collects the minimum possible
amount of extra information in addition to what is already stored in
the general ledger. In this way data collection and maintenance requirements are reduced, and it is easier to trace ABC numbers back to
the general ledger. System simplification is an important factor here.

Reporting is also a problem. The users of accounting reports
may have become accustomed to seeing the same accounting reports
for a number of years and do not want to put any effort into learning
to read new ones. Instead, they continue to use the old reports and
ignore the new ones. The obvious solution to this problem is to phase
out or restrict access to the old reports, while providing training in
the use of the new reports. Follow-up training is crucial since users
may not at first understand the concept of activity-based costing.

The trade-off between the number of cost pools used and the
level of accuracy obtained is another issue. When costs are summarized into too few cost pools, the resulting level of information accuracy is reduced, whereas an increase in the number of cost pools
(and therefore a finer level of overhead allocation) results in more
accurate costing. The trouble is that an ABC system becomes much
more expensive and complex to operate when there are too many
cost pools. To resolve this issue it is useful to create an analysis of the
incremental cost required to maintain each additional cost pool
added to the ABC model and to stop when the cost exceeds a preset
threshold or when the level of complexity appears to have become
excessive.

A final issue is that the ABC system is frequently set up to be repeated on a project basis, which means that it requires continual
reauthorization to reiterate. Because it is a project, it can be killed by
reduced funding or staffing whenever the next project renewal review occurs. ABC information is frequently derived on a project basis
because it is too expensive to collect and process on a continuing basis. To avoid this issue one can alter the ABC system so that some
parts of it are designed into the existing cost accounting system, with
some ABC information constantly being updated and only a small
part of it still obtained on a project basis. Any ABC information that
is easy to collect and interpret, or yields immediate and continuing
information of importance, can be included in the ongoing ABC sys-

tem. More peripheral ABC information can be collected on a project basis. This format retains the most crucial ABC information even if the ancillary ABC project that collects secondary data is dropped.

It is apparent that a number of issues can impede or stop the development or ongoing functioning of an ABC system. However, by using the suggestions noted here, they can all be anticipated and sidestepped, resulting in a strong, well-run ABC system that yields important accounting information.

IMPLEMENTING AN ACTIVITY-BASED COSTING SYSTEM

Though a small ABC installation can be completed by a single person in a few days, the much more likely scenario is that the installation requires a great deal of analysis, dedicated resources for a number of months, and its own budget. For this second scenario, here is a list of standard implementation steps:

1. **Obtain high-level support.** An ABC project involves the procurement of funding and dealings with multiple departments. To make these chores easier, there should be a high-level supporter of the project on the management team who can give it enough "push" through the corporate bureaucracy to ensure that it is completed in a timely manner.

2. **Obtain a project schedule and budget.** The project team leader should work with the high-level project sponsor to obtain a project schedule and funding that is sufficient for completion of the system. For organizations not familiar with ABC, this can be split into two steps, with the first step given only enough funding for a pilot project, and full funding contingent on the results of the pilot.

3. **Assemble the ABC team.** This team does not consist of just accountants. Instead, because of the wide array of knowledge required to formulate an ABC system, it should include employees from the engineering, marketing, materials management, computer services, and production departments. They may have to be assigned to the project on a full-time basis if the installation is sufficiently large.

4. **Train the team.** Many team members may never have heard of ABC before or have only a passing familiarity with it. An in-house expert or a consultant can be brought in to conduct an intensive review session with the team.

5. **Gather information.** The project team needs to gather data in order to identify activities, costs, relationships between activities and costs, and types of cost drivers. The best information is usually obtained through interviews. Additional sources of information are the general ledger, financial statements, and a detailed review of all costs. The project team can also obtain general operational information by observing operations in action.

6. **Conduct modeling and analysis.** With all the information in hand, the team should use flowcharting to determine how activities occur and flow through departments. It is at this point that resource drivers, cost pools, and activities are identified and documented.

7. **Select and purchase a software package.** It may be necessary to purchase a third-party ABC software package, which typically makes it easier to conduct analysis and ad hoc inquiries; it also makes it easier to control the system since all ABC-related files are kept in one place. The project team must assemble a detailed list of software functionality requirements and compare this list to the functionality of several possible software packages. The team should then pick the package that most closely meets its requirements.

8. **Create software linkages.** It may be possible to create automated linkages between the ABC system and other systems, such as the general ledger, that allow one to save time by streamlining the flow of information into the ABC system. These interfaces should be carefully tested to ensure their operability.

9. **Test the software.** The team should create a set of sample ABC transactions and run them through the ABC software. This step is designed not just to see if the software works as advertised but also to ensure that the team understands how the ABC system works.

10. **Design reports.** An ABC system usually requires an entirely new set of reports. These must be constructed with the ABC package's report writer, or customized, or written with the aid of a third party's software package. The team should create sample reports with test transactions to be certain that the reports function as planned.

11. **Design policies and procedures.** Once the software is determined to be acceptable, the team must prepare a set of policies and procedures to integrate the operation of the ABC system and the software into the existing operations of the accounting department. These should be tested with the people who will be using the system, and retested after the system has been installed, to ensure that they are constructed correctly.

12. **Implement the system.** The team should coordinate the training of all ABC system users just prior to the "go live" date, be present on the day the system is made operational, and, for several weeks subsequent to this date, provide a help desk to answer all user questions. Other tasks may be required during this stage, such as revisions to software code, reports, or procedures that reflect problems found subsequent to the implementation.

13. **Follow up on the installation.** An ABC system rarely works exactly as expected. Instead, there are problems that are caused by improper or inadequate training, missing procedures, or faulty analysis. To detect these problems, the project team should return to the ABC system a short time after the installation and review each of the processing steps. These problems can then be documented and corrected. Further reviews can be spread out over longer periods as the new system gradually "settles down."

Though not all these steps apply in all cases, they form a rough guide for the implementation of an ABC system. Steps can be added to or subtracted from this list to arrive at the most functional set of activities for a particular ABC installation.

BILL OF ACTIVITIES

An important outcome of an ABC system that deserves a separate discussion is the bill of activities (BOA). This document is similar to a bill of materials (BOM) in that it itemizes all the components of a product; however, it lists only the overhead components as defined through an ABC system, rather than the direct material and labor costs most commonly found in a BOM.

When combined with the costs listed in a BOM, the BOA yields a high level of detail for all costs associated with a product. These two documents then become the core of almost any cost-based analysis involving products. For example, one can use the BOA to determine the exact overhead costs to apply to a product in a full costing situation, while also assigning costs based on only certain cost pools, depending on the analysis issue being reviewed. If there is a question regarding the development cost per unit of production, the BOA has this information. If managers are curious about the overhead cost per batch, the BOA contains this information, too.

An example of a BOA is shown in Exhibit 8.4. Note that there are different line items for each cost pool, so that one can clearly differentiate the overhead costs based on batch-level, product line–level, and facility-level activities. Also, note that the cost pool quantities are divided by the activity volumes associated with these pools. For example, the product engineering cost pool is divided by

Exhibit 8.4 Bill of Activities

Overhead Cost Pool	Total Pool Cost ($)	Activity Measure	Relevant Volume	Cost per Unit ($)
Product engineering	300,000	Units produced	50,000/life cycle	6.00
Process planning	175,000	Units produced	50,000/life cycle	3.50
Batch-specific	90,000	Batch size	12,000/batch	7.50
Marketing and distribution	120,000	Annual volume	10,000/annually	12.00
Total Costs				**29.00**

the total number of units expected to be produced over the life of the product since this quantity bears a valid relationship to the research and development costs required to create it.

USES OF ACTIVITY-BASED COSTING

Now that we have an ABC system, how are we going to use it? There are many questions it can answer, such as:

- **How do we increase shareholder value?** When an ABC analysis is combined with a review of investment costs for various tactical or strategic options, one can determine the return on investment to be expected for each investment option.

- **How much does a distribution channel cost?** An ABC system can accumulate all the costs associated with a particular distribution method, which allows managers to compare this cost to the profit margins earned on sales of products sold through it. One can then determine if the distribution channel should be reconfigured or eliminated in order to improve overall levels of profitability.

- **How do product costs vary by plant?** An ABC analysis itemizes the costs of each plant and correctly allocates these costs to the activities conducted within them, which allows a company to determine which plants are more efficient than others.

- **Should we make or buy an item?** An ABC analysis includes all activity costs associated with a manufactured item, providing a comprehensive view of all costs associated with it and can then be more easily compared to the cost of a similar item that is purchased.

- **Which acquisition is a good one?** By using internal ABC analyses to determine the cost of various activities, a company can create a benchmark for these costs in potential acquisition targets. When the targets have higher costs than the benchmark levels, the acquiring company knows that it can strip out costs from the acquisition candidate by improving its processes, which may justify the cost of the acquisition.

○ **What does each activity cost?** An ABC analysis can reveal the cost of each activity within an organization. The system is really designed to trace the costs of only the most significant activities, but its design can be altered to itemize the costs of many more activities. This information can then be used to determine which activities are so expensive that they will be the main focus of management attention or can be profitably combined with other activities through process centering. This is a primary cost reduction activity.

○ **What price should we charge?** An ABC analysis reveals all the costs associated with a product and so is useful for determining the minimum price that should be charged. However, the actual price charged may be much higher since it may be driven by the ability of the market to absorb a higher price rather than the underlying cost of the product.

○ **What products should we sell?** An ABC analysis can be combined with product prices to yield a list of margins for each product sold. When sorted by market, product line, or customer, it is then easy to see which products have low or negative returns or yield such low margin volumes that they are not worth keeping.

○ **Where are the non-value-added costs?** An ABC analysis can reveal which activities contribute to the completion of products and which do not. Then, by focusing on those non-value-added activities that do not create value, a company can create significant improvements in its profitability.

○ **Where can we reduce costs?** An ABC analysis reveals the cost of anything a management team needs to know about—activities, products, or customers—which can then be sorted to see where the highest-cost items are located. Combining this with a value analysis, one can determine what costs return the lowest values and structure a cost reduction effort accordingly.

○ **Which customers do we want?** An ABC analysis can itemize the costs specific to each customer, such as special customer service or packaging, as well as increases in warranty claims or product returns. When combined with the margins on products sold to customers, this analysis reveals which customers are the most profitable after *all* costs are considered.

The number of uses to which an ABC system can be put is limited only by the imagination of the user. However, it is necessary to address this issue *before* the system is installed, for the design of the system (as noted earlier) is heavily dependent on the uses to which it will be put. To ensure that the correct system use is determined in advance, it is critical that the input of system users (especially senior-level managers) be obtained during the earliest phases of the ABC system design.

ACTIVITY-BASED MANAGEMENT

Though we have just considered the uses to which ABC can be put, they do not describe a formal methodology for using the information. This is provided by activity-based management (ABM). In essence, it begins where ABC stops by using ABC information to make changes in corporate activities that result in greater streamlining of activities.

The starting point for ABM is to determine the ratio of primary to secondary activities within an organization. A primary activity is one that contributes directly to the production of a product or service for a customer, while a secondary activity is a supporting function, such as filling out forms, entering data, calculating payroll, or issuing financial statements. It is common to see a ratio of 50:50 between these two types of activities, indicating that a large part of a company's resources are not being used in a manner that contributes to revenue production. It is the goal of ABM to drive this ratio in the direction of 100:0 (clearly impossible), usually settling for 80:20 as an indication that a company is efficient in its operations and effective in completing primary tasks.

The next step is to focus the attention of a project team on the secondary activities taking up a large part of the company's resources in terms of cost or time; time is a crucial factor if there is a significant delay in shipping products. The team carefully reviews each phase of the targeted activity, looking for wasteful steps that can be eliminated or reduced. It then works with the users of the system to see if the proposed changes will work and then designs policies and procedures that can be used as training tools and ongoing guidelines for altering the system.

Finally, the project team conducts training sessions with system users, to educate them about all the changes to be made, and then oversees the system conversion that results in a more streamlined process. The project team then lists recommended audit review steps for the internal audit team to use when it conducts its periodic audits; these steps are valuable for ensuring that the recommended changes have been firmly adopted by the system users. If not, the project team can be called in at a later date to reinforce user knowledge of the new system, perhaps with added training or slight modifications that will make it easier to operate.

This general process briefly represents how ABM works; the exact process varies by company, the composition of the project teams, and the type of system.

ROLE OF THE COST ACCOUNTANT IN AN ABC SYSTEM

The cost accountant is positioned squarely in the center of any ABC system purchase, installation, and operation. This is because the purpose of using ABC is to obtain better costing information, which is the business of the cost accountant.

The cost accountant's role in the selection of ABC software centers on the creation of a requirements definition—a listing of all the features needed in the software packages to be reviewed. The cost accountant gains this knowledge of the requirements by interviewing other employees to see what they need, as well as from their theoretical knowledge of cost accounting, knowledge of how other companies use ABC, and what the company's strategy requires in the way of costing information. This information is then assembled on a checklist which the cost accountant uses to review all prospective software selections. The best approach is to design a sample transaction that tests the presence of each requirement and then run the transaction through the sample software to see if it functions as per the itemized requirements. Because of this detailed review process, the opinion of the cost accountant is frequently the deciding factor in determining which ABC package is purchased.

Another task for the cost accountant is to structure the flow of costs through the ABC system. This involves determining what costs are to be consolidated into which costs pools and how they are to be allocated to various activities. This is information that the cost accountant deals with every day and that he has the best knowledge of. Also, the cost accountant should determine the boundaries of what will (and will not) be included in the ABC system, so that it measures only what is needed and does so within the cost budgeted for the system.

Once the system has been created, the cost accountant becomes its chief user. He determines whether any allocations require alteration, what reports it should issue, how the information is used, what employees receive information, and how this information can support strategic and tactical decisions. Since these activities nearly match a cost accountant's job description, it is evident that he must become its most expert user in order to complete his job. The ABC system and the cost accountant are closely intertwined.

CASE STUDY

The board of directors of the General Research and Instrumentation Company has completed a benchmarking comparison of the company's costs to those of its competitors and finds that the company is expending a significantly higher proportion of its revenues on production scheduling activities than anyone else in the industry; the department's costs appear to be one-third higher than they should be. It suspects that the company is running a large number of small production runs, which requires an extra scheduling effort, but wants to find out for certain before discussing operational changes with the CEO. This demand trickles down through the organization to Mr. Albert Goizueta, who is in charge of ABC analysis at the corporate headquarters. He recognizes that his main task is to determine the activities in which the production scheduling staff is involved. To do so, he assembles a planning document for an ABC system and obtains approval from the CFO, who becomes the project sponsor. Since this is a small ABC project, he requires no staff, and only a time budget for himself, so there is no need for a reallocation of resources to the project.

The next step is to construct cost pools for production scheduling. A brief review of the departmental income statement for the production scheduling department reveals that there are no costs other than payroll and benefits, which are all segregated into two separate accounts in the general ledger. Now that he knows where the underlying costs are stored, he must determine the range of activities conducted by the production schedulers and allocate these payroll costs to those activities, which are stored in separate cost pools. To locate this information he interviews the production scheduling manager, who itemizes the daily tasks along with the proportion of time spent on each one:

Activity	Proportion of Time Spent (%)
Job scheduling	32
Job under run investigation	15
Review of material shortages	53
Total	**100**

To be certain that this proportion applies to the entire production scheduling staff, Mr. Goizueta interviews the entire department and finds general agreement on the stated proportions. Then he creates a separate cost pool for each of the three main activities and allocates the salaries and benefits for the department, as itemized in the general ledger, to them. The calculation is:

Total General Ledger Cost ($)	Proportion (%)	Cost Pool Description	Allocation to Cost Pool ($)
480,000	32	Job scheduling	153,600
	15	Job investigation	72,000
	53	Material shortages review	254,400
Total	100		**480,000**

Further discussion with the production scheduling staff reveals the most appropriate activity drivers for the three cost pools. The job scheduling cost pool is entirely related to the *number of jobs* scheduled for production since a specific amount of work is required for each job to determine which machines are available, when they can be used, and how this scheduled production fits the customer's expectations. The cost pool for the investigation of jobs that were run over or under the desired quantities is most closely tied to the *number of scrapped units*, for an excessively high scrap rate results in production shortages that require the scheduling of additional production runs to complete. Finally, the material shortage review is directly tied to the *number of parts in a product*; those with a large number of component parts require much more investigation into component quantities to ensure that there are enough parts on hand for a scheduled production run. A regression analysis calculation confirms that there is a strong relationship between the activity drivers and the costs stored in the cost pools.

Mr. Goizueta's next task is to determine the total quantity of each activity driver that occurs during a standard accounting period. First, he learns that the production scheduling staff maintains a database of all production jobs, so he is easily able to compile from it a total number of scheduled jobs for the accounting period. Next he obtains from the quality assurance department the total number of scrapped units for the same period and then goes to the engineering department to obtain the number of parts required to build each product, which he then multiplies by the total number of different parts produced during the period to obtain the total number of different parts used. He then compiles this information in a table and extends it to determine the activity cost per unit of each activity driver.

Activity Driver	Activity Volume	Related Cost Pool	Total Cost in Related Cost Pool	Cost per Unit of Activity Driver ($)
No. of jobs	625	Job scheduling	153,600	245.76
No. of scrapped units	15,204	Job investigation	72,000	4.74
No. of parts in product	1,204	Material shortages review	254,400	211.30

He then needs to determine the impact of these activity costs on individual products and decides to apply the cost of each activity driver to a representative product that was running during the month under review—a wrist-mounted global positioning system (GPS). The product has direct costs of $225 and was manufactured in a production run of 450 units. The overhead costs applied to it through the ABC system are:

Activity Driver	Activity Volume in Job	Number of Units in Production Run	Cost per Unit of Activity Driver ($)	Total Unit Costs ($)
No. of jobs	1	450	245.76	0.55
No. of scrapped units	51	450	4.74	0.54
No. of parts in product	18	450	211.30	8.45
Direct cost per unit				225.00
Total				**234.54**

The last table clearly shows that the impact of the number of jobs at the current volume level per scheduled job has a negligible impact on the cost of the unit produced, as is also the case for scrapped parts that cause additional production jobs to be scheduled. The real issue is that far too many parts shortages are impacting the ability of the company to schedule and successfully complete production runs, as shown in the table by the $8.45 scheduling charge based on the number of parts contained in the product.

Armed with this ABC-based information, Mr. Goizueta can return to the board of director's original question—Why is the cost of the production scheduling department so high? The answer is contained in his report to the board:

The primary reason for the excessively high cost of production scheduling is not the size of the production runs but rather the amount of material shortages in the materials management system. The production scheduling staff must spend approximately half of its time manually verifying that materials are on hand before they can schedule production runs, which absorbs the bulk of all departmental costs. To correct this problem I recommend two steps: first, improve the materials management system with the installation of a manufacturing resources planning system that will improve the accuracy of our in-house materials records, and second, reduce the number of parts designed into our products, so that there are not only fewer components for the production scheduling staff to investigate but also fewer materials to be handled by the materials management system.

This case study shows that the use of an ABC system can reveal that the causes of costs are different than one might initially think, resulting in different management activities that can eliminate the underlying reasons for the incurrence of costs. Also, of particular interest in this case is the extremely limited nature of the study—it was designed specifically to answer a particular question, which it did in an efficient manner. Thus, implementing a broad-based, companywide ABC system may not be the answer if only specific management questions must be answered with the system—a more focused effort is more appropriate in these situations.

SUMMARY

An ABC system provides much better information about the uses of overhead costs than a traditional overhead allocation system. Though its installation must be carefully thought out to ensure that various pitfalls are avoided, an ABC system can result in a considerable improvement in the quality of cost accounting information available to a company, especially those with complex systems and multiple product lines, where costs tend to become obscured and difficult to trace to specific products, customers, or activities.

9

Target Costing

The majority of costing systems are focused on the control of labor and raw material costs and on the manner in which overhead costs are applied to production activities. However, only target costing has a tight focus on the activities that occur *before* production commences—the product design process. In this section we describe target costing and delve into the types of data it requires, as well as the situations where it can be most usefully employed. We also cover special implementation issues, points at which target costing can be most easily controlled, and the extent of its potential impact on profitability.

DESCRIPTION OF TARGET COSTING

The concept behind target costing is based on the realization that the bulk of all product costs is predetermined before a product ever reaches the production floor. This is because the types of materials used are determined during the design stage, as are the types of production methods used to shape and assemble the parts into a completed product. Consequently, the cost reduction focus of any company that designs its own products should be to closely review the costs of products while they are still in the design stage and do everything possible to keep these costs to a minimum.

The target costing method addresses the costs designed into a product with a four-step process:

1. **Conduct market research.** This involves reviewing the competitive landscape to see what other products are in the mar-

ketplace, as well as the types of new products that competitors say they are about to release into the market. It also involves a review of which customers may buy future products, what their needs are, and what prices they are likely to pay for selected product features. Further, one should determine the size of the market into which the new products are to be released and the amount of market share that can likely be obtained. This gives a company the general outlines of a revenue plan in terms of the probable number of units that can be sold and the price at which they will sell.

2. **Determine margin and cost feasibility.** This involves clarifying what product features customers want, based on the information gathered in the first step, and translating this into a preliminary set of product features that will be part of the anticipated product design. We then determine a price point, again based on the preceding market research, at which the product is likely to sell. Then we determine the standard margin to be applied to the product (which is commonly based on the corporate cost of capital, plus an additional percentage), which results in a cost figure that the product cannot exceed. We then conduct a preliminary review of anticipated product costs to see if the product design is in the cost "ballpark." If not, we cancel the design project as being unfeasible.

3. **Meet margin targets through design improvements.** This involves the completion of all value engineering needed to drive down the product's cost to the level at which the target price and margin can be attained, as well as confirming the viability of the material and process costs with suppliers and other parts of the company impacted by these design decisions. The design is then finalized, and the resulting bill of materials is sent to the purchasing staff for procurement, while the industrial engineering staff proceeds to install all required changes to the production facility needed to implement lower-cost production processes.

4. **Implement continuous improvement.** This involves the product launch at the manufacturing facility, first through a pilot production run and then at full production volumes. Also,

the cost accountant begins the regular review of all supplier costs that contribute to the cost of the product and reports variances to management to ensure that targeted cost levels are maintained subsequent to the design phase. There is also an ongoing continuous improvement program, known as kaizen costing, that focuses on the reduction of waste in the production process, thereby further lowering costs below the initial targets specified during the design phase.

These target costing steps are shown graphically in Exhibit 9.1.

A concept called value engineering was mentioned in phase 2 of the preceding process. This is a collective term for several activities used to lower the cost of a product. Here are some of the issues that are dealt with during a value engineering review:

○ **Can we eliminate functions from the production process?** This involves a detailed review of the entire manufacturing process to see if there are any steps, such as interim quality reviews, that add no value to the product. By eliminating them, one can take their associated direct or overhead costs out of the product cost. However, these functions were originally put in for a reason, so the engineering team must be careful to develop work-around steps that eliminate the need for the original functions.

○ **Can we eliminate some durability or reliability?** It is possible to design an excessive degree of sturdiness into a product. For example, a vacuum cleaner can be designed to withstand a 1-ton impact, although there is only the most vanishing chance that such an impact will ever occur; designing it to withstand an impact of 100 pounds may account for 99.999% of all probable impacts, while also eliminating a great deal of structural material from the design. However, this concept can be taken too far, resulting in a visible reduction in durability or reliability, so any designs that have had their structural integrity reduced must be thoroughly tested to ensure that they meet all design standards.

○ **Can we minimize the design?** This involves the creation of a design that uses fewer parts or has fewer features. This ap-

Exhibt 9.1 Target Costing Process

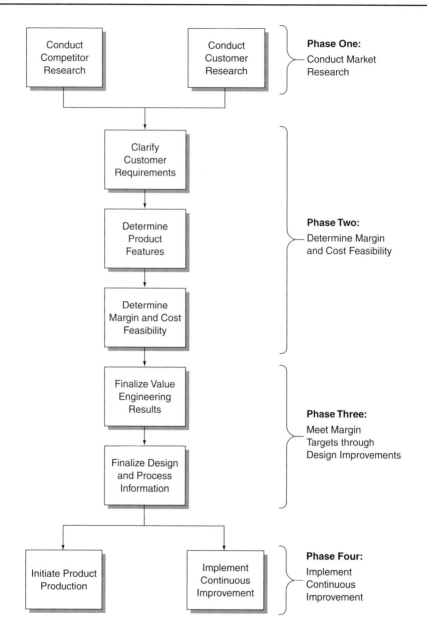

proach is based on the assumption that a minimal design is easier to manufacture and assemble. Also, with fewer parts to purchase, less procurement overhead is associated with the product. However, reducing a product to extremes, perhaps from dozens of components to just a few molded or prefabricated parts, can result in excessively high costs for these few remaining parts, since they may be so complex or custom-made in nature that it would be less expensive to settle for a few extra standard parts that are more easily and cheaply obtained.

○ **Can we design the product better for the manufacturing process?** Also known as design for manufacture and assembly (DFMA), this involves the creation of a product design that can be created in only a specific manner. For example, a toner cartridge for a laser printer is designed so that it can be successfully inserted into the printer only when the sides of the cartridge are correctly aligned with the printer opening; all other attempts to insert the cartridge will fail. When used for the assembly of an entire product, this approach ensures that a product is not incorrectly manufactured or assembled, which would call for a costly disassembly or (even worse) product recalls from customers who have already received defective goods.

○ **Can we substitute parts?** This approach encourages the search for less expensive components or materials that can replace more expensive parts currently used in a product design. It is becoming an increasingly valid approach since new materials are being developed every year. However, sometimes the use of a different material impacts the types of materials that can be used elsewhere in the product, which may result in cost increases in these other areas, for a net increase in costs. Thus, any parts substitution must be accompanied by a review of related changes elsewhere in the design. This step is also known as component parts analysis and involves one extra activity—tracking the intentions of suppliers to continue producing parts in the future; if parts will not be available, they must be eliminated from the product design.

○ **Can we combine steps?** A detailed review of all the processes associated with a product sometimes reveals that some steps can be consolidated, which may mean that one can be eliminated (as noted earlier) or that several can be accomplished by one person, rather than having people in widely disparate parts of the production process perform them. This is also known as process centering. By combining steps in this manner, we can eliminate some of the transfer and queue time from the production process, which in turn reduces the chance that parts will be damaged during these transfers.

○ **Is there a better way?** Though this step sounds rather vague, it really strikes at the core of the cost reduction issue—the other value engineering steps previously mentioned focus on incremental improvements to the existing design or production process, whereas this one is a more general attempt to start from scratch and build a new product or process that is not based in any way on preexisting ideas. Improvements resulting from this step tend to have the largest favorable impact on cost reductions but can also be the most difficult for the organization to adopt, especially if it has used other designs or systems for the production of earlier models.

Another approach to value engineering is to call on the services of a company's suppliers to assist in the cost reduction effort. These organizations are particularly suited to contribute information concerning enhanced types of technology or materials, since they may specialize in areas that a company has no information about. They may have also conducted extensive value engineering for the components they manufacture, resulting in advanced designs that a company may be able to incorporate into its new products. Suppliers may have also redesigned their production processes, or can be assisted by a company's engineers in doing so, producing cost reductions or decreased production waste that can be translated into lower component costs for the company.

A mix of all the value engineering steps noted above must be applied to each product design to ensure that the maximum permissible cost is safely reached. Also, even if a minimal amount of value engineering is needed to reach a cost goal, one should conduct the full range of value engineering analysis anyway, since this can result in further cost reductions that improve the margin of the product or allow management the option of reducing the product's price, thereby creating a problem for competitors who sell higher-priced products.

Another term mentioned in the earlier explanation of the target costing process is "kaizen costing." This is a Japanese term for a number of cost reduction steps that can be used subsequent to issuing a new product design to the factory floor. Some of the activities in the kaizen costing methodology include the elimination of waste in the production, assembly, and distribution processes, as well as the elimination of work steps in any of these areas. Though these points are also covered in the value engineering phase of target costing, the initial value engineering may not uncover all possible cost savings. Thus, kaizen costing is really designed to repeat many of the value engineering steps for as long as a product is produced, constantly refining the process and thereby stripping out extra costs. The cost reductions resulting from kaizen costing are much smaller than those achieved with value engineering but are still worth the effort since competitive pressures are likely to force down the price of a product over time, and any possible cost savings allow a company to still attain its targeted profit margins while continuing to reduce costs. This concept is illustrated in Exhibit 9.2.

Of particular interest in Exhibit 9.2 is the use of multiple generations of products to meet the challenge of gradually reducing costs. In the example the market price continues to drop over time, which forces a company to use both target and kaizen costing to reduce costs and retain its profit margin. However, prices eventually drop to the point where margins are reduced, which forces the company to develop a new product with lower initial costs (Version B in the example) and for which kaizen costing can again be used to further reduce costs. This pattern may be repeated many times as a company forces its costs down through successive generations of products. The exact timing of a switch to a new product is easy to determine well in advance since the returns from kaizen costing follow a trend line of gradually shrinking savings and prices also follow a predictable downward track; plotting these two trend lines into the future reveals when a new generation of product must be ready for production.

Exhibit 9.2 Stages of Cost Reduction

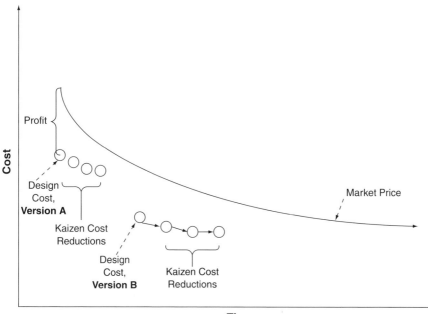

The type of cost reduction program used for target costing has an impact on the extent of cost reduction, as well as on the nature of the components used in a product. When a design team elects to set cost reduction goals by allocating specific cost reduction amounts to major components of an existing product, it tends to focus on finding ways to make incremental cost reductions rather than focusing on entirely new product configurations that might both radically alter the product's design and lower its cost. This approach is most commonly used during the redesign of products already on the market. Another cost reduction approach is to allocate cost reductions based on the presence of certain product features in a product design. This method focuses the attention of the design team away from using the same components that were used in the past, which tends to produce more radical design changes that yield greater cost savings. However, the latter approach is also a riskier one, since the resulting product concepts may not work, and also requires so much extra design work that the new design may not be completed for a long time. Therefore, the second method is generally reserved for situations where a company is trying to create products at a radically lower cost than previously.

All the changes noted in this section that are necessary for the implementation and use of the target costing methodology represent a massive change in mind-set for the product design personnel of any company because they require the constant cooperation of many departments and rapid, voluminous communications between them, not to mention heightened levels of trust in dealing with suppliers. All these concepts run counter to the traditional approach, as indicated in Exhibit 9.3.

It is no coincidence that the traditional design process shown in Exhibit 9.3 uses castles to define each of the departments that take part in the process. These departments tend to guard their turf jealously, which is a major impediment to realizing a smoothly functioning set of product development teams. Only the most active support from senior management can enforce the new approach of drawing product design team members from all these castles and having them work together amicably.

Having described the key elements of target costing, value engineering, and kaizen costing, we now turn to a variety of related topics to flesh out the reader's understanding of target costing, including target costing problems, control points, and data flows, as well as its impact on profitability and the key steps required to install it.

PROBLEMS WITH TARGET COSTING

Though the target costing system results in clear, substantial benefits in most cases, it has a few problems that one should be aware of and guard against.

The first problem is that the development process can be lengthened to a considerable extent since the design team may require a number of design iterations before it can devise a sufficiently low-cost product that meets the target cost and margin criteria. This occurrence is most common when the project manager is unwilling to "pull the plug" on a design project that cannot meet its costing goals within a reasonable time frame. Usually, if there is no evidence of

Exhibit 9.3 Traditional Product Design Process

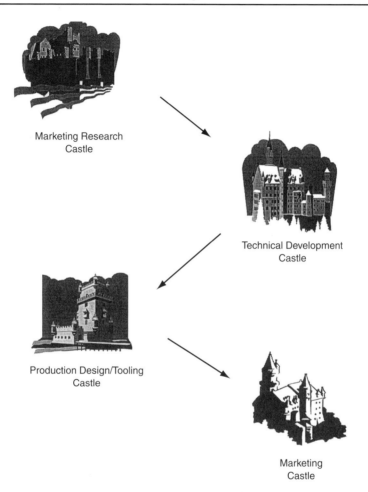

Marketing Research
Castle

Technical Development
Castle

Production Design/Tooling
Castle

Marketing
Castle

rapid progress toward a specific target cost within a relatively short amount of time, it is better to either ditch a project or at least shelve it for a short time and then try again, on the assumption that new cost reduction methods or less expensive materials will be available in the near future that will make the target cost an achievable one.

Another problem with target costing is that a large amount of mandatory cost cutting can result in finger-pointing in various parts of the company, especially if employees in one area feel they are being called on to provide a disproportionately large part of the savings. For example, the industrial engineering staff will not be happy if it is required to completely alter the production layout in order to generate cost savings, while the purchasing staff is not required to make any cost reductions through supplier negotiations. Avoiding this problem requires strong interpersonal and negotiation skills on the part of the project manager.

Finally, having representatives from a number of departments on the design team can sometimes make it more difficult to reach a consensus on the proper design because there are too many opinions regarding design issues. This is a major problem when there are particularly stubborn people on the design team who are holding out for specific product features. Resolving this difficulty requires a strong team manager, as well as a long-term commitment on the part of a company to weed out those who are not willing to act in the best interests of the team.

For every problem area outlined here, the dominant solution is retaining strong control over the design teams, which calls for a good team leader. This person must have an exceptional knowledge of the design process, good interpersonal skills, and a commitment to staying within both time and cost budgets for a design project.

COST ACCOUNTANT'S ROLE IN A TARGET COSTING ENVIRONMENT

Given the strong cost orientation in a target costing environment, there is obviously a considerable role for the cost accountant on a design team. What are the specific activities and required skills of this person?

The cost accountant should be able to provide for the other members of the design team a running series of cost estimates based on initial design sketches, activity-based costing reviews of production processes, and "best guess" costing information from suppliers based on estimated production volumes. Especially in the earliest stages of a design, the cost accountant works with vague cost information and so must be able to provide estimates within a high-low range of costs, gradually tightening this estimated cost range as more information becomes available.

The cost accountant should also be responsible for any capital budgeting requests generated by the design team since he or she has the most knowledge of the capital budgeting process, how to fill out the required forms, and precisely what types of equipment are needed for the anticipated product design. The cost accountant also becomes the key contact on the design team for answers to any questions from the finance staff regarding issues or uncertainties in the capital budgeting proposal.

The cost accountant should work with the design team to help it understand the nature of various costs (i.e., cost allocations based on an activity-based costing system), as well as the cost-benefit trade-offs of using different design or cost options in the new product.

In addition, the cost accountant is responsible for tracking the gap between the current cost of a product design and the target cost that is the design team's goal, providing an itemization of where cost savings have already been achieved and where there has not been a sufficient degree of progress.

Finally, the cost accountant must continue to compare a product's actual cost to the target cost after the design is completed, and for as long as the company sells the product. This is a necessary step because management must know immediately if costs are increasing beyond budgeted levels and why these increases are occurring.

Given the large number of activities for which a cost accountant is responsible under the target costing methodology, it is evident that the job is a full-time one for all but the smallest costing projects. Accordingly, a cost accountant is commonly sent to a design team as a long-term assignment and may even report to the design team's manager, with few or no ties back to the accounting department. This may even be a different career track for a cost accountant—permanent attachment to a series of design teams.

There are particular qualifications that a cost accountant must have to be assigned to a target costing team. Certainly, one is having a good knowledge of company products as well as their features and components. Also, the cost accountant must know how to create an activity-based costing system to evaluate related production costs, or at least interpret such costing data developed by someone else. Further, he or she must work well in a team environment, proactively assisting other members of the team in constantly evaluating the costs of new design concepts. In addition, he or she should have good analytical and presentation skills, since the ongoing costing results must be continually presented not only to other members of the team but also to the members of the milestone review committee (see "Target Costing Control Points"). Thus, the best cost accountant for this position is an outgoing person with several years of experience within a company or industry.

IMPACT OF TARGET COSTING ON PROFITABILITY

Target costing can have a startlingly large positive impact on profitability, depending on the commitment of management to its use, the constant involvement of cost accountants in all phases of a product's life cycle, and the type of strategy a company follows.

Target costing improves profitability in two ways. First, it places such a detailed continuing emphasis on product costs throughout the life cycle of every product that it is unlikely that a company will experience runaway costs; also, the management team is completely aware of costing issues since it receives regular reports from the cost accounting members of all design teams. Second, it improves profitability through precise targeting of the correct prices at which the company feels it can field a profitable product in the marketplace that will sell in a robust manner. This is opposed to the more common cost-plus approach under which a company builds a product, determines its cost, tacks on a profit, and then does not understand why its resoundingly high price does not attract buyers. Thus, target costing results not only in better cost control but also in better price control.

Target costing is really part of a larger concept called concurrent engineering, which requires participants from many departments to work together on project teams rather than having separate departments handle new product designs only after they have been handed off from the preceding department in the design chain. Clustering representatives from many departments together on a single design team can be quite a struggle, especially for older companies that have a history of conflict between departments. Consequently, only the most involved, prolonged support by all members of the senior management group can ensure that target costing, and the greater concept of concurrent engineering, will result in significant profitability improvements.

The review of product costs under the target costing methodology is not reserved just for the period up to the completion of design work on a new product. On the contrary, there are always opportunities to control costs after the design phase is completed, though these opportunities are fewer than during the design phase. Therefore, cost accountants should not be pulled from a design team once the final drawings have left the engineering department. Instead, they should regularly monitor actual component costs and compare them to planned costs, warning management whenever significant adverse variances arise. Also, cost accountants should take a lead role in the continuing review of supplier costs to see if they can be reduced, perhaps by visiting supplier facilities, as well as constantly reviewing existing product designs to see if they can be improved, and by targeting for elimination waste or spoilage on the production floor. Therefore, the cost accounting staff must be involved in all phases of a product's life cycle if a company is to realize profitability improvements from target costing to the fullest extent.

A company's strategy can also impact its profitability. If it constantly issues a stream of new products, or if its existing product line is subject to severe pricing pressure, it must make target costing a central part of its strategy so that the correct price points are used for products and actual costs match those originally planned. However, there are other strategies, such as growth by geographical expansion of the current product line (as is practiced by retail stores) or growth by acquisition, where there is no particular need for target costing—these companies make their money in other ways than by a focused concentration on product features and costs. For them, there may still be a role for target costing, but it is strictly limited by the reduced need for new products.

If the issues presented here are properly dealt with by a management team, it should find that target costing is one of the best accounting methods available for improving profitability. It is indeed one of the most proactive systems found in the entire range of accounting knowledge.

TARGET COSTING DATA FLOW

The typical accountant is used to extracting data from a central accounting database carefully stocked with the most accurate, reliable data from such a variety of sources as accounts payable, billings, bills

of materials, and inventory records. However, the cost accountant assigned to a target costing project must deal with much more poorly
defined information, as well as data drawn from sources much different from those he or she is accustomed to using.

In the earliest stages of product design, the cost accountant
must make the best possible guesses regarding the costs of proposed
designs. Information about these costs can be garnered through the
careful review of possible component parts, as well as a comparison
to the costs of existing products with designs similar to those now
under review. No matter what the method, it results in relatively
rough cost estimates, especially during the earliest stages of product
development. To operate in this environment a cost accountant
must have a wide-ranging view of costing systems and a willingness to
start with rough estimates and gradually refine them into more concrete information as designs gradually solidify. Therefore, cost accountants with a narrow focus should not be assigned to a product
design team.

Though cost estimates are admittedly rough in the earliest stages
of a new product design, it is possible to include with the *best* estimate
an additional estimate of the *highest* possible cost that will be encountered. This additional information lets management know whether
there is a significant degree of risk that the project may not achieve
its desired cost target. Though this information can result in outright
termination of a project, it is much more common for senior management to interview the project director in some detail to gain a better understanding of the variables underlying an excessively high cost
estimate, as well as the chances that these costs can be reduced back
to within the targeted range. Only after obtaining this additional information should a company make the decision to cancel a product
design project.

There are also new sources of data a cost accountant can access.
One is competitor information collected by the marketing staff or an
outside research agency. This database contains information about
the prices at which competitors are selling their products, as well as
the prices of ancillary products and perhaps also the discounts given
at various price points. It can also include market share data for individual products or by firm, the opinions of customers regarding the
offerings of various companies, and the financial condition of com-

petitors. This information is mostly used to determine the range of price points at which a company should sell its existing or anticipated products, as well as the features that should be included at each price point. The information about the financial condition and market shares of competitors can also be of use, since a company can elect to alter the pricing of its products to obtain a better market position. This database is of value to the cost accountant in determining the price at which products should be released to the market.

Another database used by the cost accountant is one that details the cost structure of competitors. This information is compiled by a combined effort of the marketing and engineering staffs through a process called reverse engineering. Under this methodology a company buys a competitor's product and disassembles it in order to determine the processes and materials used to create it, and their costs. This information is of value in determining the greatest allowable cost of a new product design since a company can copy the methods and materials used by a competitor and see if a reduction in costs will be achieved. The information is also of use from a pricing perspective since it gives management some idea of the profits a competitor is probably obtaining from sales of its products; management can then aggressively price some or all of its competing products low enough to take away some of the competitor's profits.

Cost data can be found in yet another database that the cost accountant should peruse. This is not the inventory or bill of materials data already available in the typical accounting database but rather costs associated with specific product features or the production functions involved in manufacturing them. This type of information is not commonly found in the accounting system. Instead, the engineering staff may have compiled, over the course of numerous design projects, a set of tables itemizing the cost of components or clusters of components used to create a specific product feature. Also, the cost of specific production functions generally requires an in-depth analysis that can be obtained only through a prolonged activity-based accounting review. If none of this information is available, an enterprising cost accountant assigned to a product design team may take it upon herself to conduct this research, thereby not only improving the costing database of the current product design team but also providing a valuable information base for future design teams.

Yet another database is one containing engineering data. This information does not stop with the usual bills of materials and also includes notes on upcoming technological changes that can be used to enhance the features of existing products. There should also be information about the interaction of various components of a product, so that one can predict what cost changes are likely to arise in the subsystem of a product if a part is reconfigured in a different subsystem. Further, there should be information available about the changes in costs that will arise from the use of a smaller or larger number of fasteners, different materials, different product sizes or weights, or a host of other factors. All this information is not easily reduced to a standard database format, and so it tends to be partly paper-based and not as well organized as the information stored in other databases. Nonetheless, this is a valuable tool for the cost accountant since it yields many clues regarding how costs can be altered as a result of changes in product design.

The final database available to the cost accounting member of a design team contains information regarding the previous quality, cost, and on-time delivery performance of all key suppliers, as well as the production capacity of each one. It may even reach a sufficient level of detail to include assumed profitability levels for each supplier. The cost accountant can use this information to determine which standard parts are no longer acceptable for future product designs, based on a history of high cost, poor quality, or inadequate on-time delivery. Also, if suppliers clearly show inadequate profits, it may signal their inability to obtain further cost reductions through capital asset purchases, which may necessitate switching to a different supplier.

Based on the wide variety of data sources mentioned in this section, it is evident that the cost accountant who is an integral member of a product design team has access to a considerable amount of information that is of great use in determining product prices and costs. However, few of these data sources are those that the typical accountant is used to accessing, nor do they contain the high level of data accuracy more common in an accounting database. Consequently, the cost accountant who collects this information must be well trained in its uses, as well as its shortcomings, and be able to use it to realistically portray expected cost and margin levels, given its imprecise nature.

MOST USEFUL SITUATIONS FOR TARGET COSTING

Target costing is most useful in situations where the majority of product costs are locked in during the product design phase. This is the case for most manufactured products, but few services. In the services arena, such as consulting, the bulk of all activities can be reconfigured for cost reduction during the "production" phase, which is when services are being provided directly to the customer. In the services environment the "design team" is still present but is more commonly concerned with streamlining the activities conducted by the employees providing the service, which can continue to be enhanced at any time, not just when the initial services process is being laid out.

For example, a design team can lay out the floor plan of a fast-food restaurant, with the objective of creating an arrangement that allows employees to cover the shortest possible distances while preparing food and serving customers; this is similar to the design of a new product. However, unlike a product design, this layout can be readily altered at any time if the design team can arrive at a better layout, so that the restaurant staff can continue to experience high levels of productivity improvement even after the initial design and layout of the facility. In this situation costs are not locked in during the design phase, so there is less need for target costing.

Another situation where target costing results in less value is the production of raw materials, such as chemicals. In this case there are no design features for a design team to labor over; instead, the industrial engineering staff tries to create the most efficient possible production process, which has little to do with cost reduction through the improvement of customer value by creating a product with a high ratio of features to costs.

TARGET COSTING CONTROL POINTS

A target costing program eventually results in major cost reductions if design teams are given an unlimited amount of time to carry out a multitude of design iterations. However, there comes a point where the cost of maintaining the design team exceeds the savings to be garnered from additional iterations. Also, most products must be released within a reasonably short time frame or they will miss the appropriate market window when they can beat the delivery of competing products to the market. To avoid both these cost and time delays, we use milestones as the principal control point over the course of a target costing program.

Several milestone reviews should be incorporated into a target costing program. Each one should include a thorough analysis of the progress of the design team since the last review, such as a comparison of the current cost of a design with its target cost. The main issue here is that the amount of cost yet to be worked out of a product must shrink, on a dollar or a percentage basis, after each successive milestone review, or else management has the right to cancel the design project. For example, there may be a standard allowable cost variance of 12% for the first milestone meeting, 10% at the next meeting, and so on until the target cost must be reached by a specific future milestone date. If a design team cannot quite reach its target cost, but comes close, the management team should be required to make a "go/no go" decision at that time which overrides the cost target and sends the design into production, allows time for additional design iterations, or terminates the project.

A milestone can be based on a time budget (e.g., one per month) or on the points in the design process at which specific activities are completed. For example, a milestone review can occur as soon as each successive design iteration is completed, when the conceptual drawings are finished, when the working model has been created, or when the production pilot has been run. In the last-mentioned case, there are many more steps that the management group can build into the milestone review process so that cost analyses become a nearly continual part of the target costing regimen.

IMPLEMENTING A TARGET COSTING SYSTEM

A target costing initiative requires the participation of several departments. Because there are so many participants in the process from so many departments, some of whom have different agendas in regard to what they want the program to produce, it is quite common for the results obtained to be less than stellar. Design projects can be delayed by squabbling or by an inability to drive down design or production costs in a reasonably efficient manner. This delay may lead to serious cost overruns in the cost of the design team itself, which can lead to abrupt termination of the entire target costing system by the management team. However, these problems can be mitigated or completely eliminated by ensuring that the steps listed here are completed when the target costing system is first installed:

○ **Create a project charter.** The target costing effort should begin with a document, approved by senior management, that describes its goals and what it is authorized to do. This document, known as the project charter, is essentially a subset of the corporate mission statement and related goals as they pertain to the target costing initiative. Written approval of this document by the senior management group provides the target costing effort with a strong basis of support and direction in all subsequent efforts.

○ **Obtain a management sponsor.** The next step is to obtain the strongest possible support from a management sponsor. This should be an individual who is well positioned near the top of the corporate hierarchy, believes strongly in the goals of target costing, and will support the initiative in all respects—obtaining funding, lobbying other members of top management, working to eliminate roadblocks, and ensuring that other problems are overcome in a timely manner. This person is central to the success of target costing.

○ **Obtain a budget.** The target costing program requires funds to ensure that one or more well-staffed design teams can complete target costing tasks. The funding should be based on a formal allocation of money through the corporate budget, rather than a parsimonious suballocation grudgingly granted by one or more departments. In the first case the funds are unreservedly given to the target costing effort, whereas in the latter case they can be suddenly withdrawn by a department manager who is not fully persuaded of the need for target costing or who suddenly finds a need for the money elsewhere.

○ **Assign a strong team manager.** Because the typical target costing program involves so many people with different backgrounds and represents so many parts of a company, it can be difficult to weld the group together into a smoothly functioning team focused on key objectives. The best way to ensure that the team functions properly is to assign to the effort a strong team manager skilled in dealing with management, the use of project tools, and working with a diverse group of people. This manager should be a full-time employee, so that his or her complete attention can be directed toward the welfare of the project.

○ **Enroll full-time participants.** A target costing team member puts the greatest effort into the program when he or she is focused only on target costing. Thus, it is essential that as many members of the team as possible be devoted to it full-time rather than also trying to fulfill other commitments elsewhere in the company at the same time. This may call for the replacement of these individuals in the departments they are leaving so that there are no emergencies requiring their sudden withdrawal back to their "home" departments to deal with other work problems. It may even be necessary to permanently assign them to a target costing program, providing them with a single focus on ensuring the success of the target costing program because their livelihoods are now tied to it.

○ **Use project management tools.** Target costing can be a highly complex effort, especially for high-cost products with many features and components. To ensure that the project stays on track, the team should use all available project management tools, such as Microsoft Project (for tracking the completion of specific tasks), a company database containing various types of costing information, and a variety of product design tools. All these items require assured access to many corporate databases, as well as a budget for whatever computing equipment is needed to access this data.

The main focus of the steps described in this section is to ensure the fullest possible support for target costing by all available means—management, money, and staff. Only when all these elements are in place and concentrated on the goals at hand does a target costing program have the greatest chance for success.

CASE STUDY

The GetLost Company is a manufacturer of global positioning systems (GPS) used in a variety of applications to determine a user's precise position on the surface of the planet. The founder of the company, Mr. Larry Ost, is concerned that the price point for hand-held recreational GPS units has plummeted from more than $500 to about $100 in the past five years in response to severe pricing pressure from competitors. He decides to attack the problem by creating a target costing team.

The team conducts a number of marketing surveys to determine what features a prospective GPS unit should include. It finds that a key complaint of potential users is that all GPS units currently on the market are too bulky, which is a major concern for hikers and hunters who want to reduce the size of anything they carry with them into the outdoors. In a major insight the marketing personnel on the team decide to combine the GPS unit with a standard walkie-talkie, which many outdoorsmen also carry. The resulting device can then be marketed as a major space saver compared to the alternative, which is to carry both devices.

On initial review, the target costing team compiles a set of costs for a device that will cost $200, well above the $125 that surveys reveal is the most realistic price point for this type of device. Also, since the company wants to attain a 25% margin on this product, the team arrives at a cost reduction goal of $106 in this manner:

Target market price	$125
Target margin	25%
Target margin	$ 31
Target cost	$ 94
Current cost	$200
Target cost	–$ 94
Cost reduction goal	$106

To meet the cost reduction goal, the team begins its value engineering effort by reviewing combined functions in the radio and GPS parts of the product. It finds that both share an antenna and a receiver; by merging these two components the company can save $45. Also, by working with a supplier the team finds that a new liquid crystal display (LCD) is now available that can cut the price of the existing LCD by $40. Finally, a design review of the circuitry in the product reveals that microminiaturization will result in a $2 cut in the price of the circuit board, while also creating a board that is half the size of its predecessor. This allows the design team to create a much smaller plastic case for the device, reducing both the molding cost for the case and the cost of creating the injection mold used to create the case. The cost reduction from these two innovations is $19. All these changes yield a new product cost of $94, which allows the GetLost Company to produce an innovative new product in a highly competitive market—and one that carries with it a reasonable profit.

As a final measure, the target costing team assigns several staff members to review the production process with the objective of eliminating enough production waste to further reduce costs by 3% per year on a continual basis. Achieving this goal will allow the company to continue to reduce prices in the future, in the face of a heightened level of expected competition, while still retaining a reasonable degree of profitability.

SUMMARY

Target costing is one of the few "proactive" costing activities an accounting department performs. Most other costing work done by accountants involves an after-the-fact review of costs that have already been incurred. Only in this case does the cost accountant form an active part of the new product design team, constantly apprising the design team of the current cost of a design, as well as the impact of contemplated design changes on costs. These activities have a major direct impact on the profitability of products, which makes target costing, and the cost accountant's role in it, one of the most valuable activities a company can pursue.

In this chapter we discussed the various steps a target costing program typically follows, as well as the types of value engineering that can be used to remove costs from a product design and the production processes used to manufacture it. We also noted the situations in which target costing is most useful, how it impacts profitability, where to install control points over the process, and how to implement the methodology.

10

Costing Systems Summary

So far we have looked at nine methods for summarizing and interpreting costing information. Each one can be effectively used in specific circumstances, but may provide useless, or incorrect, information in others. In this chapter we briefly review each of these costing systems and then discuss the situations in which each one should be used.

BRIEF REVIEW OF COSTING SYSTEMS

This section presents a summary of each of the costing systems discussed in the first nine chapters of this book. Each summary includes a description of the system, the cost accountant's role in its use, and how the resulting information is generally used.

Job costing is one of the most common systems used to track a company's costs. As many costs as possible are directly tied to specific jobs on which a company is working, while most other costs are summarized into cost pools and then allocated to the jobs. This approach makes up the bulk of a company's data collection systems since most costs must be tracked in some way to an overhead cost pool or to a job; this requires the use of job tracking for employee labor hours and material costs. The cost accountant is responsible for setting up and maintaining the job costing system, as well as for investigating any unusual cost amounts charged to specific jobs. This method is useful for determining the full cost of each production job, especially when these costs can be billed directly to a customer.

Process costing is used almost as frequently as job costing. It requires the collection of data for long production runs in which individual units cannot be readily distinguished from fellow products (i.e, in oil refining) or for production runs that are so long that it is difficult to determine the start and stop intervals for a specific job within an accounting period. It involves the aggregation of cost data into cost pools, which are then spread across the total volume of production during a specified period. As was the case for the job costing system, the cost accountant must set up and maintain the system, as well as investigate any apparent discrepancies in cost accumulations or allocations. This approach is used for generating approximate per-unit costs, as well as inventory valuations.

Direct costing deals with only a portion of a company's total costs. It collects data only about costs that can be directly and indisputably assigned to a specific product or activity and charges all other costs to the current period. This makes for a simpler data collection system since there is no need to compile or allocate overhead costs. The cost accountant's role in its use is similar to that for job and process costing. It is most commonly used for determining the minimum price point at which an item can be sold.

Standard costing assumes that actual costs vary only slightly from period to period, thereby allowing standard costs to be substituted for them. In this way actual costs can be compared to the standards, and variances generated and investigated. The cost accountant has considerable work to do in this system because the job expands to include variance investigation. This system works best in cases where a company has been in business for some time and therefore has a cost structure that does not vary much from period to period.

LIFO, FIFO, and average costing are all different ways to model the flow of costs through a company. When the correct calculation method is used, a slightly more accurate view of how costs flow can result. Since each of these costing methods is automatically maintained by the accounting computer system, the cost accountant's role is limited to investigating any unusual changes in costing layers. Each of these systems is most commonly used to value inventory for external reporting purposes.

Throughput costing differs substantially from every other costing system in that it does not involve *any* costs—it focuses only on the in-

cremental gross margin generated by a company's bottleneck operation. It assumes that changes in costs elsewhere in a company do not
have a substantial impact on bottom-line profits, so only decisions regarding the product mix at the bottleneck point have any relevance.
In this system, the cost accountant's role is altered substantially, to
that of a capacity analyst. This method has many uses, particularly for
determining incremental changes in the production mix.

Joint and by-product costing is a set of allocation methods used to
assign costs to two or more products jointly created by the same
production process. Being strictly an allocation system, it is best
used only for inventory valuations or external financial reporting
where *some* sort of cost allocation is required. The cost accountant
performs the allocation calculations and justifies their formulation
with a company's outside auditors.

Activity-based costing is a complex system that charges direct materials and labor to specific products, while also charging overhead
costs to a series of cost pools; these pools are then allocated to various activities in the production process, which are in turn used as the
basis for cost allocations to specific products. The focus of the ABC
system is generally on product costing, but it can be refocused on
specific company processes, customers, or anything else about which
costing information is required. It is a highly detailed system that
seeks to allocate *all* costs in as comprehensive a manner as possible so
that the recipients of the resulting information have the best possible
information about the complete set of costs incurred by a product.
The cost accountant is deeply involved in the setup and maintenance
of this system, which requires many detailed analyses, data collection
systems, and calculations.

Target costing involves the ongoing accumulation of costs for new
products currently under development and the use of this information to determine if such products can be manufactured at a target
cost that will generate sufficient profit to make the development effort worthwhile. This system may not result in perfectly accurate costs
since many of them are estimates, obtained internally or from suppliers, that may vary somewhat as each development project proceeds.
However, the costs should become more accurate over time as the
costing information for each development project becomes more certain. Thus, the cost accountant must continually refine the accuracy

of the costing information supplied to the design team. This information can be used to make a decision to abandon or to proceed with a project, as well as to focus on the specific parts of a development project that require cost reductions in order to meet the cost target.

Having briefly described each of the costing methodologies, we now proceed to review the situations in which each one is most useful.

APPLICATIONS OF COSTING SYSTEMS

There are a number of decisions to which a cost accountant can contribute valuable information—information that can be derived from a combination of the various costing systems. In this section we itemize the most important cost-related decisions and point out which of the various systems can be best used to support them. The results are also listed in a table in Exhibit 10.1, which highlights the particular uses of each costing system. The main costing decisions involve:

- ○ **Capacity utilization.** From the perspective of capital investment, the management team needs to know what assets are under- or overutilized so that it can change the mix of equipment being employed on the shop floor. This is particularly important for bottleneck operations since sales cannot be increased to a higher level than can be run through the operation. Only the throughput costing system targets this issue. It assumes that the main focus of management attention should be the amount of revenue that can be rammed through the bottleneck operation, so it pays close attention to which work center is the bottleneck and how well this machine is used. However, even throughput costing is really concerned only with the bottleneck operation rather than with the capacity utilization of all other work centers, so a special data gathering system must typically be constructed to track this information.

- ○ **Capital budgeting.** The main goal of capital budgeting is to determine the cash inflows and outflows associated with a specific capital purchase. The direct costing system is particularly

Exhibit 10.1 Uses of Costing Systems

Costing System	Capacity Utilization	Capital Budgeting	Cost Reduction	External Financial Reporting	Internal Management Reporting	Inventory Valuation	Outsourcing Decisions	Pricing	Process Improvement	Product Design	Product Mix	Product Profitability Costing	Scrap Costing
Job costing			X	X		X		X				X	
Process costing				X		X		X				X	
Direct costing		X			X		X	X					
Standard costing								X	X			X	X
LIFO, FIFO, average costing				X		X							
Throughput costing	X		X		X		X	X	X		X		X
Joint and by-product costing			X	X		X							
Activity-based costing			X	X	X	X		X	X			X	X
Target costing			X		X			X		X		X	

useful for this function since it focuses specifically on costs that can be directly traced to a single activity (in this case, a machine), while excluding all other nonrelevant costs. Other systems, such as job, process, and activity-based costing, all allocate overhead costs, which may not be relevant to a capital budgeting decision. Thus, these other systems are less likely to reveal relevant information for this purpose.

○ **Cost reductions.** The perennial favorite question asked by all managers is: How can the company save money? Several systems can be used to answer this question, depending on the precise nature of the question. For example, if the question is oriented toward how to save money on manufactured products, the best method to use is target costing; this system closely tracks costs as a product is being developed and so can influence final product costs considerably. If the question is oriented more toward nonproduct costs, the best alternatives are job and activity-based costing. Job costing is (as the name implies) oriented toward costs incurred to complete a job and so provides good costing detail at that level. An ABC system, however, focuses on overhead costs and how they are used by various activities. When employed properly, the ABC system can provide a wealth of detail in this area. Finally, throughput costing can be used to determine whether changes in costs will impact the ability of a bottleneck operation to manufacture more or fewer products—in some instances this system results in recommendations to increase rather than decrease costs on the grounds that an incremental cost increase may result in a higher level of throughput and therefore a higher gross margin (Chapter 6).

○ **External financial reporting.** This item has less to do with supporting management decisions and more with following a fixed set of accounting rules in order to issue a reliable, accurate set of financial statements. For this purpose a cost flow system such as LIFO, FIFO, or average costing should be used to create a legally correct inventory valuation. We should also use the job, process, joint and by-product, or ABC system to allocate overhead in a legally valid manner.

We cannot use the direct costing system because it does not provide for overhead allocation, nor can throughput or target costing be used since they are specialized applications not oriented toward this use.

○ **Internal management reporting.** This is a broad topic that may require a wide range of systems to ensure that valid information is provided to solve numerous possible problems. Generally speaking, the costing systems employed to generate external reports are *not* the ones to use for internal reports because the overhead allocations needed for external reporting are less useful for internal reporting. Thus, we favor direct, throughput, ABC (the one system that is useful for both internal and external reporting because of the accuracy of its overhead allocations), and target costing systems for internal reports.

○ **Inventory valuation.** The valuation of inventory requires the allocation of costs to inventory items because this is required by generally accepted accounting principles. This requirement immediately reduces our choices to a few systems that incorporate allocation methodologies, namely, the job, process, cost flow (e.g., LIFO, FIFO, and average costing), joint and by-product, and activity-based costing systems. Indeed, some systems, such as joint and by-product costing, are designed almost entirely for this use.

○ **Outsourcing decisions.** Any decision to shift an in-house function to an outside supplier requires an incremental analysis of how this change will affect a company's costs. For incremental analysis there is nothing better than direct costing since this system avoids the use of all costs that do not directly pertain to a cost object. Another good system for outsourcing decision making is throughput costing because it can tell if outsourcing will alter the total amount of product that can be pushed through a company's primary bottleneck operation, thereby impacting gross margins.

○ **Pricing.** One area in which the cost accountant is likely to become involved is the setting of product prices. Sales and marketing managers, who set prices, want to know the fully burdened cost of each product so that they can determine a price point that will cover all costs over the long term. For this purpose one can use the job, process, standard, and activity-based costing systems. In addition, there are incremental pricing situations in which they want to know the minimum price that can be charged—for this, the direct costing system is the best alternative. Also, if there is a problem with pricing products that must flow through a bottleneck operation, the throughput costing approach is the best methodology. Finally, if product pricing is a methodical process in which new products are carefully designed to meet a specific price point, the best alternative is target costing. Unfortunately for the cost accountant, nearly every costing system can be used for pricing simply because there are so many variations on how to set a price.

○ **Process improvement.** Three systems can be used for process improvement analysis, though each one is employed for entirely different purposes within this category. First, direct costing is used to determine the incremental cost of a particular process activity. It is used to develop a minimum cost for a process step that will change if a process improvement is implemented. This is the most common costing method for this purpose. The second system is throughput costing, which can be employed to determine what gross margin changes can be expected if any process improvements are made that will impact a bottleneck operation. This procedure is used the least because many process improvement efforts bear no relationship to a bottleneck operation, which means that throughput costing is indifferent to them. Third, activity-based costing is used to improve processes that require a large amount of overhead costs. It is ideal for this purpose because it carefully tracks how overhead costs are used by various activities—by reducing the activities, the related overhead costs can (theoretically) also be eliminated. Thus, different systems can be used for different purposes under the general heading of "process improvement."

○ **Product design.** Without a doubt the only costing system to use for product design analysis is target costing. This system was specifically created to trace the ongoing costs of new product designs in relation to target cost levels and so is the perfect vehicle for conveying product design costing information to the management team.

○ **Product mix.** The decision to manufacture a specific mix of products is the primary purpose for creation of the throughput costing system, which clearly identifies how changes in the production mix influence the total gross margin that can be expected. Other costing systems do not yield such excellent results because they "muddy the waters" by using overhead cost allocations, which usually have no direct relevance to the product mix decision.

○ **Product profit.** There are many ways to determine how much of a profit a product has earned. If a fully burdened profit is the objective, then the job, process, standard, joint and by-product, or activity-based costing system should be used. However, if the incremental profit earned from product sales is the desired result, direct costing is the preferred alternative. Finally, if the management team simply wants to verify that the planned profit for a new product is being met in the marketplace, target costing can be used. Thus, one must be conversant with many different costing systems to know how to properly report product profitability.

○ **Scrap costing.** Different systems yield entirely different costing results in the valuation of manufacturing scrap. On one hand, an activity-based costing system values it based on the amount of overhead it has absorbed, as well as all direct costs. On the other hand, a throughput costing system places a higher value on scrap downstream from a bottleneck operation because it must be replaced with good production that must be run through the expensive bottleneck operation again. Finally, a standard costing system works best for segregating excess scrap from a standard use rate, which makes it easier to determine where high scrap levels are occurring. The most commonly used of these systems is standard costing because it gives higher visibility to scrap costs. However, throughput costing is recommended as an ancillary system because it highlights the increased cost of downstream scrap.

A graphical view of the preceding costing system applications is presented in Exhibit 10.1, where the various costing systems are displayed in the first column and the various costing decisions just discussed are shown as column heads.

A key issue to remember from this discussion of system applications is that no one system can be used in all situations since each one is designed for a different purpose. If a single system were used, its results would be correct for some applications but seriously incorrect for others. Not only would this constantly cause trouble for the management team, which would make incorrect decisions based on incorrect costing reports, but it would also reduce the perceived effectiveness of the cost accountant within the organization.

SUMMARY

As indicated in Exhibit 10.1, there are many uses to which costing information can be put. No single costing system can meet all these demands. Some are good at costing for a single purpose, while others have broader applicability. However, it is simply not possible to use one system for all of a company's costing needs. Consequently, the cost accountant must have a broad knowledge of all the systems mentioned here and know when to use different systems in different situations.

Index

Index

V

Variance analysis, 51

W

Weighted average method
    Process costing data flow, 18–21

Getting to Know Him

*Let us know, Let us pursue the knowledge of the Lord. His going forth
is established as the morning; He will come to us like the rain, Like
the latter and former rain to the earth.*—Hosea 6:3 NKJV

Not too long ago, a young man who had recently been converted
asked me, "How can I grow faster? There is so much to learn and know,
and I want to move forward." It is so exciting to see this kind of enthusiasm in an individual. Certainly, not everyone who is saved is as eager to
change. Nevertheless, one can grow only as quickly as the Spirit allows. It
is the Spirit who leads and guides us into all truth.

It is the daily seeking to know God that brings real change. We keep
the lines open to the Spirit, saying, "God, what do you want to reveal to
me today?" Then, as we listen with our hearts, we may hear his voice gen-
tly speak one word, maybe a phrase, which at the time may not seem
earthshaking. But it is these little daily revelations that over time bring a
greater knowledge of our Lord. We build our knowledge of him one picture at a time, much like our earthly relationships are constructed.

We get to know someone as we share bits of time, gaining glimpses
into his or her heart that gradually build into a "knowing" that gets
stronger and stronger each time we're together. Similarly, God does not
reveal himself to us all at once. For one thing, we simply cannot hold all
of who God is. Even the great apostle Paul, after years of knowing God,
said he would know him only like "a poor reflection as in a mirror" until
he could see him face to face and know him "fully" (1 Cor. 13:12).

Do not despair at the learning process if it seems slow. Enjoy the journey, the getting there, the discovering of his mercies that come new with
every day (see Lam. 3:23). There are glorious revelations awaiting anyone
who seeks him diligently, listening intently to the ordinary for the supernatural.

∞

Lord, what are you saying to me today? What revelation are you bringing to
my spirit? Open my understanding and let me rejoice in each discovery, knowing that each treasure is a gift from you. What a joy it is to get to know you
by looking in what seems commonplace and finding the secrets of your glory.

endurance

Ready...Set...Go!

Those who live according to the sinful nature have their minds set on what that nature desires; but those who live in accordance with the Spirit have their minds set on what the Spirit desires.—Romans 8:5

Battle units that are thoroughly trained, frequently drilled, and always ready for action have a much better chance of survival when the enemy strikes than units that don't make preparedness a priority. A unit may have the latest weapons at its disposal, but if the soldiers are not battle-ready, a surprise attack can easily wipe them out.

Most Christians know that when we are born again, we become new creatures. What some do not realize, however, is that when we are born again, it is our spirit beings that come to life. The rest of who we are—body and soul—must die to its former nature. The mind's transformation comes when we use our wills to apply the principles in the Scriptures. The old passions and thought patterns must be cast down so that we can live by God's Word.

I've found that one of the best ways to carry out this transformation is to set my mind "on what the Spirit desires" as soon as I open my eyes each morning, before I even get out of bed. I make a conscious effort to "look to Jesus" to find the spiritual energy I'm going to need for the victories of the coming day. By following this strategy, I find that when the sinful nature cries out and conjures up its carnal passions and desires, my mind is fortified against them and better prepared to reject what is not "in accordance with the Spirit."

Let us follow the advice of the apostle Peter, who wrote, "Therefore, prepare your minds for action; be self-controlled; set your hope fully on the grace to be given you when Jesus Christ is revealed" (1 Pet. 1:13). Let's get ready for battle!

❦

Lord, keep me determined to prepare my mind for action. Help me to be in control of myself and to have my heart fully set on what the Spirit desires. I want to be armed and ready for the battle, confident that I will overcome. I will be victorious!

No Shortcuts in the Kingdom

Everyone who competes in the games goes into strict training. They do it to get a crown that will not last; but we do it to get a crown that will last forever.—1 Corinthians 9:25

Most men I know would choose a shortcut to get anywhere they're going. If there is a quicker way to get somewhere, you can be sure a man is going to use it. I know because I am one, and I have been known to take what appeared to be a shortcut only to find myself taking twice as long to get where I was going.

Every day we are inundated with shortcuts to a goal: "Get-rich-quick" schemes. "Lose thirty pounds in thirty days!" "Learn a foreign language in twelve easy lessons." Usually, as the saying goes, if it sounds too good to be true, it probably is.

Life is full of shortcuts—real and false. But there are no shortcuts to becoming a godly man or woman. It is God's way or no way. Wouldn't it be great if there were such a thing as one-step maturity? Then there would be no journey of faith, no spiritual mountains, and no adversity. Just a quick prayer and *swoop!* it would be done.

There are no such shortcuts. But that doesn't mean they won't be offered to us. You can be assured that sooner or later every man or woman of God will be tempted with an easy way to spiritual maturity. The enemy of our souls is all too happy to try and lure us into such a pursuit.

The way to godliness is training. And yet it is not the training itself that makes us godly. The training merely polishes the windows of our souls so the cleansing power of God can shine through and change us. God is the real key to godliness. If we could make ourselves godly, we wouldn't need a Savior. Only God can make us godly.

⌘

Lord, I'm committed to staying in training. I pray that your character will show through me as I stay on the path you have chosen for me.

endurance

Weekend Reflections

"In the Christian life, it's not how you start, it's how you finish. Your level of endurance is important," says Steve Farrar in his book *Point Man*. As Christians we endure difficulties because we know the end of the story. Jesus endured the cross for the joy (see Heb. 12:2). Paul pressed on for the prize (see Phil. 3:14). What hardships are you enduring? What joy do you anticipate?

1. Jesus was offered a shortcut instead of enduring the cross. How is yielding to temptation a shortcut that leads to emptiness?

   _____

   _____

   _____

   _____

   _____

2. The best things in life are most often the things that require us to work or endure. How is this similar to the life of the believer?

   _____

   _____

   _____

   _____

   _____

3. A runner must train to endure the strain of the marathon. What can you do to strengthen your spiritual endurance?

   _____

   _____

   _____

   _____

   _____

Walking Between the Lines

See to it that no one takes you captive through hollow and deceptive philosophy, which depends on human tradition and the basic principles of this world rather than on Christ.—Colossians 2:8

The Christian walk at times may seem like walking between the lines, bouncing off the bumpers of grace and self-righteousness. On one side is the vain effort of man to measure up to the awesome righteousness of all that is truly holy. On the other is the ever-abounding grace of God.

It is comforting to know we are not alone in this struggle. The apostle Paul wrote two very different letters to Galatia and Corinth. The church at Galatia had chosen the path of the Judaizers and were falling into the trap of the old regulations and traditions. On the other hand, the Corinthian believers had all sorts of immorality among them, and Paul rebuked them sharply.

How do we bring the two together? How do we walk in grace and follow his command, "Be ye holy for I am holy" (1 Pet. 1:16 KJV)?

In the key verse above, Paul cites the hollowness and deception of worldly philosophy, "which depends on human tradition and the basic principles of this world rather than on Christ." In other words, the principles may look good, but they are hollow when it comes to working effectively unless they center and totally rely on Christ and his power to work within.

It all comes back to Christ and the power of his death, burial, and resurrection working in and through us. As songwriter Robert Lowry penned so effectively, "This is all my hope and peace, nothing but the blood of Jesus. This is all my righteousness, nothing but the blood of Jesus."

So we look to Jesus. To nothing or no one else. We set our affections on him, as Paul said (see Col. 3:2 KJV). Only in him do we find the power to walk between the lines.

❧

Lord Jesus, you have called us to be holy people, and it is your presence in me that gives me the power to be holy. I make a decision today to be numbered among those people. Thank you for your grace as I continue to press on.

holiness

The Great Exchange

For he hath made him to be sin for us, who knew no sin; that we might be made the righteousness of God in him.—2 Corinthians 5:21 KJV

One of the powerful mysteries of the Bible is how, when we come to Christ in repentance, God takes our sin away and gives us his righteousness in exchange. Our bodies become God's temples, and the parts of our bodies become the members of Christ's body.

Growing up, when someone in my family was sick, my mother would put the ailing one to bed and keep the door to that room closed. She sprayed disinfectant until the whole house smelled like a hospital, and she changed the bed linens frequently, washing everything in the hottest water she could stand because she wanted to kill the germs and keep the illness from spreading to the rest of the family.

When we come to Christ, we become one with him (see 1 Cor. 6:17). The "sickness" of our sin is laid upon him, and it becomes his sickness. In exchange, his righteousness becomes ours. The diseased self is consumed by the broken body of Jesus, and we receive in our spiritual veins a transfusion of the holy blood of Christ that gives life to the new self created in his image. As Paul said, "If anyone is in Christ he is a new creation; the old has gone, the new has come!" (2 Cor. 5:17). So we do not join ourselves to the "sickness" of unbelievers, because doing so would make us participants in their sin. Instead, we join ourselves to Christ, and through this holy union he receives our sin and gives us the gift of himself.

∞

Lord Jesus, you are worthy of praise, for you not only cover our sin but actually take it away! By faith I believe that my sin has already been laid upon you and I have received the gift of your righteousness in exchange.

Starving the Old Man

For when I am weak, then I am strong.—2 Corinthians 12:10

To be strong in the Lord is to be weak in the flesh. Most of us try to understand and follow this principle, but it is not always easy. How do we remain strong in the Lord on a continual rather than a temporary basis? How do we live victoriously week in and week out?

To live a Christlike life is to die to the old nature. We know this is true; it isn't a new theology. But we all find it harder to apply this principle than to understand it. I find it helps to think of this "dying to the old nature" as "starving the old man."

In an extended fast, the first seven days or so are the most difficult. The stomach groans and complains, as if it is a child begging for food. Then, after the first week, the body begins to quiet down and gradually gives up its complaining. Though the desire for food is still there, it is much easier to deal with.

The same is true in the spiritual realm. As we starve the old carnal affections, they gradually become less demanding, less difficult to control. At the same time, as we nourish our spiritual side, becoming like Jesus becomes a natural instinct.

Like hunger that decreases but lingers in one who is fasting, our worldly desires are still there, even when we think we have them under control. So we should not become discouraged if we fail. Self-discipline takes time. It is a process of reeducation, as we learn to be patient with ourselves just as Christ is patient with us. As we starve our old natures, we unreservedly draw nourishment from his inexhaustible strength. And soon we find ourselves feasting at God's overflowing table of love and goodness.

Lord, feed me with your love and power so that I can resist the old affections steadfastly, rejoicing in my life as a new creation in you.

holiness

He Emptied Himself

Jesus was in the stern, sleeping on a cushion.—Mark 4:38

The picture of Christ, the Son of God, sleeping soundly in a boat being tossed about by a tempest is thought provoking. Divinity at rest while the winds howl and men scurry about trying to adjust rigging and bail water just doesn't seem natural.

But that is in fact what it was. It was *natural*. Though Jesus was God, he was also a man whose *natural* body got weary and needed a nap now and then. His body was no different from yours or mine.

This dichotomy is something that confounds the wise. How was he God and yet man? How is it that he "emptied Himself," as the apostle Paul says, and yet remained God? (Phil. 2:7 NASB).

It wasn't that he emptied himself of his power. The power was available to him twenty-four hours a day. But he chose to confine himself to the limitations of a mortal human body. One paraphrase of Philippians 2:7 reads, "He set aside the privileges of deity and took on the status of a slave"(THE MESSAGE). He did this for our sakes so that he could know how it feels to be a man, so he could "sympathize with our weaknesses"(Heb. 4:15).

Suppose you were handicapped and had to walk with crutches. If I, a person with healthy legs, were to walk with crutches alongside you, it would be because I chose to do so. Though I would have the power to walk freely without the crutches, I would choose the limitation for myself. That is what Christ did. He chose to limit himself to the frailties of the human body, even though he had the power to supernaturally live in perfection. He laid aside his own rights and became a servant, obedient to the cross.

How do we follow him in this? By not always demanding our own rights and choosing instead to serve those around us. To suffer with those who suffer. To weep with those who weep. We choose to understand, so that we might be understood.

∞

Lord, thank you for emptying yourself for us, for setting aside your divine privileges to become fully human. You know what it is to feel weariness, loss, and grief as well as pure joy. Help me to be aware of the times when I am selfishly demanding my own rights at the expense of others.

Follow the Man Who Walks with a Limp

The sun rose above him as he passed Peniel, and he was limping because of his hip.—Genesis 32:31

Jacob left Peniel a different man than he had come. Much more than a physical change took place that day. Yes, Jacob walked differently the rest of his life after his encounter with God at Peniel, but an even bigger change occurred inside his heart. Jacob faced his greatest fear and the result of his most seedy act of deception. Instead of deceiving himself anymore and rather than assuming he could weasel out of a tight situation one more time, at Peniel Jacob faced his fears alone with God. And he left as a man truly aware of his dependence on his Creator.

I've heard it said, "Don't follow a man who doesn't walk with a limp." I have often used that bit of advice in choosing the people with whom I would have long-term associations. Show me someone who is successful and has never experienced any defeat or failure, and then show me someone who has triumphed over disappointment, fear, or failure, and ask me which person I would follow into the storm. Always, my answer is the same: I'd follow the one who walks with a limp. Who wants to follow someone has never faced his or her greatest enemy, the false self? Who will follow a person who has never trembled in the darkness, never cried, never been afraid? Is he really a leader to be followed?

Holiness is forged in the fires of battle. Some of the most mature men and women of God have waged the tough battle and have emerged stronger and more holy, yet encumbered by a limp. These are the men and women who know Christ more intimately because they have shared with him in his suffering (see Rom. 8:17).

❧

Jesus, you are the ultimate example of a man unashamed of his scars. Let me bear the marks of one who has walked with you.

holiness

Weekend Reflections

Of all the names God uses to describe himself, one of my favorites is *Holy*. According to one Hebrew source, it generally means "set apart, consecrated." To many, the holiness of God is a subject full of dread and fear. But as children of God, we should have a *holy* fear for God, not a *dreadful* fear. His wrath has been appeased through the work of the Cross (see 1 Thess. 5:9).

1. Is the holiness of God something you fear? If so, why?

_____

_____

_____

_____

_____

2. What would be the dangers of serving a God who was not holy?

_____

_____

_____

_____

_____

3. How can we be holy as he has commanded us to be?

_____

_____

_____

_____

_____

Belonging to Christ

If you belonged to the world, it would love you as its own. As it is, you do not belong to the world, but I have chosen you out of the world. That is why the world hates you.—John 15:19

In relationships there are different levels of commitment. For example, at work, the employer-to-employee relationship is based on the employee's level of performance. The boss promises, "As long as you carry out your responsibilities, I will see that you are compensated." In friendships outside the workplace, relationships may be based on a commitment to sharing common interests and having somewhat the same view on life. Unfortunately, for too many couples, the marriage relationship is a commitment to stay in the marriage until one of the spouses gets bored with the arrangement.

Our relationship to Christ is different from these earthly commitments. When we say we belong to him, we're talking about a long-term, lifetime commitment. God has made a covenant with us. He is committed to seeing us through the process of becoming more like him until Christ's nature is completely formed in us. Even when we are ready to give up on ourselves, God never gives up on us. His words should forever ring in our hearts: "Can a mother forget the baby at her breast and have no compassion on the child she has borne? Though she may forget, I will not forget you! See, I have engraved you on the palms of my hands" (Isa. 49:15–16).

∞

Lord, I praise you for your unfailing love. There is never a time that you have forgotten about me. Thank you for being that kind of God!

TUESDAY

He'll Never Let You Go

*It is the Lord Who goes before you; He will [march] with you; He will
not fail you or let you go or forsake you; [let there be no cowardice or
flinching, but] fear not, neither become broken [in spirit] (depressed,
dismayed and unnerved with alarm).*
—Deuteronomy 31:8 AMPLIFIED

These were the words of Moses to his beloved friend and aide, Joshua.
Moses knew his death was approaching. Now Joshua would have to lead
the people into the Promised Land. He would have to finish what Moses
could not do.

Joshua needed Moses' firm words of encouragement. He needed to be
told again that God would be with him just as he had been with Moses.
He needed that same assurance that God would remain faithful.

When we face changes in life, we often start grasping for what we feel
is secure, something that will not change. We may look to a trusted loved
one, such as a spouse, mother, or father, or to an older mentor or a long-
time friend. In times of radical change, such as the death of a spouse or a
child, we desperately cling to the One who will not change. Like Joshua,
we need to hear again the words of Moses, to be told again that God "will
not fail you or let you go."

There is no arm as strong as our God's, no hand that grips so surely.
He has a firm hold on you, and he will never let you go. No matter where
you go, no matter what you may face, no matter what changes come.

❧

Father, thank you for the times when words were insufficient and you just held
me. You are the foundation that stands secure. I will run to you in time of trouble and hide in the shadow of your wings (see Ps. 57:1).

One on One

But Noah found grace in the eyes of the Lord.
—Genesis 6:8 KJV

Before God destroyed the earth with the great flood, he saw a corrupt world, the wickedness of man. Everywhere God looked he saw rebellion and depravity—everywhere, that is, except in one man: Noah. God saved Noah and his family because of Noah's faithfulness.

When we consider God's greatness, his immeasurable power and ability, the idea that he can see us as individuals seems out of reach. It is easier to think of God as One who relates to us corporately rather than one on one. The fact is, though, that God knows us individually, just as he knew Noah. And he loves each of us in our own right. Each one of us is special to him.

Consider this as your challenge: Realize the vastness of God's mental capacity; it's greater than anything you can ever imagine, big enough to manage a universe. And yet God's mind can linger with you at any time. We may have difficulty doing two things at once, but God is bigger. He can do *all* things at once—and still know us as intimately as a Creator knows his creation.

To God, no one job requires any more effort than another. Nothing is a task. He is in perfect control of this cosmos, and he still has time to listen and keep his eyes on you.

❧

Lord, there is not a time that I am out of your sight. I am not a statistic or number in your kingdom but a child that you know by name.

Does God Sleep In on Mondays?

Behold, he that keepeth Israel shall neither slumber nor sleep.—Psalm 121:4 KJV

Oh, those Sundays! The worship days when the very heavens seem to open and God seems close enough to touch, when we shake the rafters with our Lord's Day songs of praise. Oh, what glorious Sundays they are!

Then comes Monday, and suddenly we feel so terribly unspiritual.

From time to time all of us struggle to sense the supernatural in the ordinary daily grind, especially, it seems, on Mondays. We long to see the miraculous in the mediocre, to bring a little Sunday heaven into the week-day blahs, but sometimes it's awfully hard to do. Do you ever wonder if God hides from us on Mondays?

No, he is there on our moody Mondays as well as our super Tuesdays, wonderful Wednesdays, troublesome Thursdays, and frustrated Fridays. He doesn't live at church. He isn't with us only when we are feeling spiritual; he's our Friend, our Spirit, our Comforter twenty-four hours a day, seven days a week. His mercies are new every morning.

Sometimes we want to put God and his love and glory in a nice little package and leave it at church. After all, we reason, God is too holy to go with us to our secular jobs where we mingle with sinners. When I start thinking that way, I remember what Oswald Chambers said: "There is no division between sacred and secular, it is all one great glorious life" *(Our Brilliant Heritage)*.

I believe God included the Song of Solomon in the Bible, if for no other reason, to let us know he is the author of all that is truly good in life. He is there with us through it all. In our joy, he smiles with us. In our sadness, he weeps with us. He is a God who is intimately involved in the routine humdrum of our daily lives as well as the intricate workings of the cosmos. Even on Monday mornings. Because God never sleeps in.

⮑

Oh Lord Jesus, open my heart to sense you in the everyday, to walk by faith when there is no feeling. I know in my heart that what you have said is true. You are there whether or not I sense your presence. It is your faithfulness, oh God, that keeps us together, not my feelings.

God Is Not Surprised!

Dear friends, don't be surprised at the fiery trials you are going through, as if something strange were happening to you.—1 Peter 4:12 NLT

Sometimes life catches us unaware and jolts us into believing that our lives are spinning out of control. The chaos may be brought on by an unexpected loss or a sudden change in the seasons of life. Maybe we find ourselves with an unexpected child, or maybe we find ourselves suddenly childless. Maybe our children head off to college or our spouses head off into midlife crisis.

I recall one dear saint who asked for prayer one day after a midweek Bible study. With tearful emotion she said, "I don't know what to do. My children are grown and have their own lives now. When they were at home, I knew my purpose was to be the best mother I could. I worked hard to raise them in the knowledge of the Lord. But now they're gone, and I don't know why I'm here."

I felt great compassion and wondered what I could say to encourage her and help relieve her distress. Then, in a few moments, I heard that small voice inside me saying, "Tell her I am not surprised."

The depth of meaning in those few words brought great comfort to her—and to myself as well. Although we might be surprised by the circumstances that swirl through our lives, God is not. He is always ahead of us, preparing the way, ordering our steps. He is never caught off guard. Never will we hear him say, "What do I do now?" Instead, he lovingly holds our hands and leads us. "Walk on, child," he tells us. "I know you're surprised, but I'm not. I know the plan I have for you, and you are going to be just fine!"

No matter how chaotic it may feel, your life is not out of control. If you are walking in covenant with God, he will be faithful. He knows where you are; he has ordered the steps of your life (see Ps. 37:23 KJV). He knows the path you will take, and he is not anxious or weary.

❦

Oh Father, your ways are higher. What comfort it is to know that although I may be surprised occasionally by my circumstances, you are never shocked or startled at life. You know the path I take, and I cannot escape from your presence. I know you have plans to prosper me.

Weekend Reflections

Questions will come. Voices will call us to doubt God's faithfulness. But when worry torments us, we should stop and realize that the One whose purpose we are questioning is the One who hung the stars on nothing, carved the landscape with his word, and breathed our spirits into existence. How can we expect to completely understand his methods when we behold his genius, his omnipotence in all he has performed?

1. Look at nature and identify how creation points to God's faithfulness (for example, the rainbow, the seasons, the stars).

   _____

   _____

   _____

   _____

2. The apostle Paul said, "The one who calls you is faithful and he will do it" (1 Thess. 5:24). What has God called you to do? How are you leaning on his faithfulness to "do it"?

   _____

   _____

   _____

   _____

   _____

3. Faithfulness depends on character. God will keep *his* part of the covenant. What is *your* part? (See 2 Chron. 6:14.)

   _____

   _____

   _____

   _____

   _____

The Terrible World of the Ungrateful

But mark this: There will be terrible times in the last days. People will be lovers of themselves, lovers of money, boastful, proud, abusive, disobedient to their parents, ungrateful, unholy.—2 Timothy 3:1–2

It almost seems a little unfair, doesn't it, to include the ungrateful with such disreputable company as the proud, the abusive, and the disobedient? When we think of terrible times, we wouldn't normally expect the ungrateful to be blamed for contributing to such conditions.

Yet Paul, describing a scene of gross immorality and depraved minds, included among the sins of men who were "without excuse" (Rom. 1:20) the fact that they "neither were thankful" (v. 21 KJV).

We all know people who are never thankful. Who enjoys the company of such people? Their ungratefulness spills over into their general attitude toward life.

Corrie ten Boom learned the power of thankfulness in the comfortless conditions of a flea-infested prison camp. In her book *The Hiding Place,* she said that one day she and her sister, Betsie, were reading 1 Thessalonians 5:18—"In every thing give thanks" (KJV)—when Betsie encouraged her to give thanks for the fleas. It was only after her sister's persistence over several months that Corrie finally relented and thanked God for the pests. Sometime later they learned that they had been able to study the Bible and pray without interference because the guards would not enter the barracks due to the fleas.

Are you having a problem with gloominess and despair? Try expressing more gratitude, first to God and then to others. Sit down and make a list of the things in your life you can be thankful for. Then pray your thanks aloud. Your ears need to hear it too!

Start with gratitude for breath to live. For freedom. For a God who loves you and looks forward to being with you.

❧

Father, I choose to be thankful today. You are a gracious God whose love endures forever. Great is your faithfulness to me.

TUESDAY

Holding On with a Loose Grip

Instead, you ought to say, "If it is the Lord's will, we will live and do this or that."—James 4:15

The longer I live the more I have come to believe that nothing is permanent—except maybe "permanent press." Everything else is subject to change. The sooner we realize this, the less life will take us by surprise.

When it comes to life and people, anything can happen. It is a mistake to base your life on the present set of circumstances. Go ahead and make plans, but realize there may have to be some adjustments. The sooner you can accept this fact, the sooner your life will be governed by peace. James advised that we should say, "If it is the Lord's will, we will live and do this or that" (v. 15). This is the proper way to make plans.

God is a God of vision and purpose. He wants us to set goals and make plans—as long as we recognize his sovereignty as the highest authority. Remember: "Many are the plans in a man's heart, but it is the Lord's purpose that prevails" (Prov. 19:21).

Whether it is wealth, children, or a job, all our blessings are gifts from God. We must enjoy them today, because only God knows about tomorrow. Corrie ten Boom said, "I've learned that we must hold everything loosely, because when I grip it tightly, it hurts when the Father pries my fingers loose and takes it from me!" (*Living above the Level of Mediocrity*, Chuck Swindoll).

If you are going to grip anything tightly, let it be the hand of God. Hold everything else with an open hand. Then if your other hand becomes empty, your balance will remain steady because you are holding something that never changes.

⸏

Father, I recognize your sovereignty today. You alone know the future and what it may hold. I submit my plans to you, and I pray your will be done. The earth and its fullness are yours, including everything you have given to me. Family, friends, and things are all gifts that you have allowed me to hold for a little while.

What Kind of House Are You Building?

If any man builds on this foundation using gold, silver, costly stones, wood, hay or straw, his work will be shown for what it is, because the Day will bring it to light. It will be revealed with fire, and the fire will test the quality of each man's work.—1 Corinthians 3:12–13

Although I have never experienced having my home destroyed by fire, I have witnessed a few such fires in the small town where I was raised. There wasn't a whole lot of excitement, so when there was a fire, everyone came to watch.

I remember one particular fire that consumed a classmate's home. As I stood beside the girl whose home it was and watched it burn, she wept not for the house so much as for things that couldn't be replaced. "Pictures," I heard her say. When the fire finally burned itself out, only the stone foundation and a pile of twisted metal pipes remained.

Throughout our lifetimes, you and I are building houses, but they are houses we cannot really see with natural eyes. From time to time we get a glimpse of the evidence of the houses, but there is only One who truly sees them. One day, though, we will know for certain what we have used to build our houses, whether we have built them with the things that will endure or with temporary pleasures. We will know whether we have used gold and silver or wood and straw "because the Day will bring it to light." God will test it with his fire on the day of judgment. Those things done for the praise of men or for selfish gain will be burned up. That's the wood and straw. But whatever is done for the glory of God will stand and remain.

Next time you do something you think is of value, ask yourself, *Is this wood and hay, or is it gold and silver?* Have you stopped to look at your spiritual house?

∞

Oh God, I want to build things that will last, that will stand through the test of your fire. Don't let me waste time on houses of hay and stubble. Make the motives of my own heart evident to me.

thanksgiving

Embrace It!

Be thankful.—Colossians 3:15

Life certainly does not always go as we plan. But that's part of God's plan! As Oswald Chambers said in *So I Send You*, "According to the Bible, things do not go as we expect them to." While some things are sure in the Christian life—salvation, God's faithfulness, daily provision, heaven—there are other things we may dream of that will never happen. And if we knew all things, we probably would thank God that he did not give us everything we dreamed of! "If God had granted all the silly prayers I've made in my life," wrote C. S. Lewis, "where should I be now?" *(Letters to Malcolm).*

Don't postpone your life until some perfect time or place in the future. That time or place may never come. Don't put off getting involved in a church until you find the perfect congregation "where people are more loving and committed." Don't put off living, thinking *If I just had a different spouse...*or *If only I could be shorter, taller, thinner...* I am not making light of these desires. I know these issues have brought much heartache to some people. But, my friend, the truth is that God is God of the present. For whatever reason, he has allowed you to be at this place and time with these circumstances, and his peace will come to us when we embrace life in the here and now.

Like Little Orphan Annie, you might be singing, "The sun will come out tomorrow." And it's true: Your situation may change. Your dreams may all come true. But if the sun doesn't come out, if your dreams don't come true, live *today* anyway. Do all you can to enjoy this moment God has given you. Be thankful for it! Embrace it!

∞

Lord God, you are my Father. I must admit I don't always understand, but I thank you for what you have given me here and now. I will not wait for the future but will live and find the beauty in today.

Have You Heard the Secret?

I know what it is to be in need, and I know what it is to have plenty.
I have learned the secret of being content in any and every situation,
whether well fed or hungry, whether living in plenty or in want.
—Philippians 4:12

It's true: Expenses rise to meet income. It's so easy to feel that whatever we have is never enough. We get a raise, then we buy more stuff. Then we need another raise to pay for the maintenance of the new stuff. So we buy some maintenance stuff to take care of the old stuff. Then you need another raise to maintain the new maintenance stuff…and the cycle goes on.

In contrast to this endless cycle of want, the trademark of the godly person is contentment. Whether this person has little or much, he or she finds a way to be at peace.

This is not something that just happens, like receiving salvation or being healed. It is something a godly person *learns*. Even the great apostle Paul said, "I have *learned* the secret." Paul knew what it was like to have plenty of "stuff," and he knew what it was like to need stuff. And in both places he found a secret.

What secret of contentment was he is referring to? It was the fact that he was strengthened by Christ himself: "I can do everything through him who gives me strength" (Phil. 4:13). Now it is no longer a secret. Paul has shared his knowledge with us.

Though I may not know how to do it yet, I am *learning* to be content—whether I have a lot of stuff or I think I need a few more things.

∞

Father, sometimes I think I know what I need, but only you really know, and you know before I ask. You graciously supply my needs according to your great riches. I thank you for teaching me contentment in all things. Whether I abound or lack, you strengthen me so that I am satisfied with you.

thanksgiving

Weekend Reflections

Gerald Mann wrote, "In every tragedy you can look at what you've lost and be hateful, or you can look at what you have left and be grateful. Joseph (Old Testament) was a grand example of choosing to be grateful instead of hateful in the face of betrayal" *(When the Bad Times Are Over for God)*.

There is a cure for those afflicted with the disease of self-pity. It's called *thankfulness*. It is by expressing thanks for what we *do* have that our eyes are lifted from ourselves to what is lovely, good, and right. Suddenly what we don't have or what we cannot have loses its power over us, and we find the courage to be a giver and not just a receiver.

1. Spend an hour writing down everything you are thankful for. Gauge the difference in your attitude before and after.

_____

_____

_____

_____

2. Think of those who seem to be the most joyful and content. How big a part does thankfulness play in their lives? What about those who are miserable?

_____

_____

_____

3. How does being unthankful lead to a more sinful state? (see Rom. 1:21–32).

_____

_____

_____

_____

Just Say No

For the grace of God that brings salvation has appeared to all men. It teaches us to say "No" to ungodliness and worldly passions, and to live self-controlled, upright and godly lives in this present age.
—Titus 2:11–12

One of the first words we try to teach children to understand is the word *no*. From the moment they eagerly look at those basement steps, we earnestly hope they will quickly learn to obey.

I was watching a good friend of mine attempt to teach his two-year-old the significance of this word as the child repeatedly tried to stick things into the electrical outlets. Unfortunately, the word *no* didn't suffice, and when Dad wasn't looking the child got a shocking surprise! The youngster learned the advantages of obedience the hard way. Much like that little child, we sometimes fail to heed the voice of God in our hearts saying no as he tries to teach us lessons for living.

The word *teaches,* as found in Titus 2:11, is translated from a word that means "to train up a child, to educate." We are God's children, learning to be more like him, but we're still in training. We are not there yet. Like my friend's little child, we hear God's voice in our heart, but sometimes we just don't listen. Or perhaps we can't quite accept that God is right; we can't see how this one little thing could be wrong. And we set ourselves up to learn a lesson the hard way.

The self-controlled, upright, and godly life awaits us; it is something we earnestly reach for as his grace continues to instruct and guide us in saying no to worldly passions—those passions that war within and without. If we heed God's voice instructing us, we do not have to learn the hard way; nor do we have to be burned by the enemy's fire. God, in his grace, is working diligently within us to keep and to protect us from the evil one in this present world. He is teaching us to obey...by saying no.

∞

Father, thank you for your grace that patiently teaches us. Give me ears to hear and a heart that readily obeys your voice. Teach me that sometimes all I need to do is just say no. Keep me from the evil one. Let me walk circumspectly, aware of the enemy's devices.

growth

Forward Ho!

*Being confident of this, that he who began a good work in you will
carry it on to completion until the day of
Christ Jesus.*—Philippians 1:6

I have always been fascinated by the clipper ship. There is something so free and inviting about the vessel's grand sails, stretched taut, welcoming the winds of the sea. The ship doesn't sail under its own power, so there's no engine noise. Just the sound of the sails snapping out in the breeze and the splashes of the hull skimming across the waves of the briny deep.

We should remember that, like the clipper ship, we do not move under our own power but the power of the Holy Spirit. We just exert our wills—lift our sails—to be controlled by the Spirit's leading. As Paul wrote, "If we live by the [Holy] Spirit, let us also walk by the Spirit. [If by the Holy Spirit we have our life in God, let us go forward walking in line, our conduct controlled by the Spirit]" (Gal. 5:25 AMPLIFIED).

Have you longed to reach a point in your life when you feel complete as a Christian, fulfilled and enriched with God's plan for your life? Have you ever felt frustrated, thinking, *I'll never get there?* Take heart in the apostle's words to the Philippians: "He who began a good work in you will carry it on to completion."

Lift your sails, open your heart, and let the Spirit move you toward completion. God's purpose in your life will be fulfilled; your destiny will be realized; it will be completed! God is seeing to it that the work that was begun carries on day by day until the prize is obtained, the destination is reached.

If your goal is to become like Jesus, God is working in you to see that you attain that goal.

∞

Father, I believe that you are working in me today, carrying on the work that you started. I believe that I will see the day when your work is completed and a new one is begun and that together we will walk forward from glory to glory.

growth

From Ordinary to Extraordinary

For those God foreknew he also predestined to be conformed to the likeness of his Son, that he might be the firstborn among many brothers.—Romans 8:29

Before a sculptor ever begins to sculpt, he or she has a picture in mind of what the end will be. Everything the artist does to the stone or wood as he or she chips and chisels away conforms to that mental image of the end product. God works the same way in our lives. When he sees us, he sees us with the end in mind.

This is why Jesus called as his disciples such ordinary men—not the scholars and wise men of the day but seemingly common men who had an extraordinary propensity to *become*. Jesus saw their potential, saw what they could be. He looked at Peter and said, "Upon this rock I will build my church; and the gates of hell shall not prevail against it" (Matt.16:18 KJV). Peter is the same man Jesus rebukes a few verses later for his hasty speech. Jesus saw Peter's weaknesses, but he also saw the giant of a man who would one day be willing to give his life for the Gospel.

If we could only see the end of our lives as well as the present! If we could only realize the power that is working in us and understand what it's capable of doing in our lives! The greatness of this power is incomparable. It is the same power that raised Jesus from the dead! Just imagine: That power is alive and working in us right now, conforming us to the heavenly design and purpose that God has fashioned.

∞

Father, your purpose for me is what I want. You have the ending of my story in mind, but I know it's up to me to choose to embrace your plan for me. I pray that you will guide me in the path that leads to my heavenly calling.

growth

Come On In!

All that the Father giveth me shall come to me; and him that cometh to me I will in no wise cast out.—John 6:37 KJV

Did you ever have one of *those* teachers when you were in school? You know, the ones who simply refused to help? Who denied that you could be having trouble understanding? "Don't worry about it," he or she would say. "Just hang in there; you'll get it." How fortunate we are that our heavenly teacher is not that way. When we boldly come before the throne of grace, he smiles and says, "Come on in!" In contrast to those teachers and friends who are intolerant of our slow progress, Jesus is patient, "full of compassion, and gracious, longsuffering, and plenteous in mercy and truth" (Ps. 86:15 KJV).

It is interesting to note that the Greek word translated as "no wise" in John 6:37 is *ou nay,* a double negative. Jesus was saying emphatically, "I will never, no never, reject one of them who comes to Me" (AMPLIFIED).

"God, I was just here a few hours ago," we say apologetically. "I'm sorry, Lord. I'm back again. I...I didn't get it." But we don't have to apologize. We consider time and space differently than God does. Time is not an issue with him. So if we come to the Lord twenty times in a single day, it's not a nuisance to him. He realizes our helpless state. That is why he came to earth, to empower us to do what we could not do ourselves.

Yes, it is humbling to admit our weaknesses, but it should always be a joy to come to the throne of grace. God is glorified in our weakness. It is in our needful state that his strength is revealed.

∞

Lord Jesus, I choose to come to your throne of grace. Where else can I go? Your kindness draws me to you (see Rom. 2:4).

Grow Up? But How?

Like newborn babies, crave pure spiritual milk, so that by it you may grow up in your salvation.—1 Peter 2:2

Children are children because that is all they know how to be. No matter how frustrated parents become with their children, the children cannot become adults until the appointed time. They will continue to make mistakes and think only of themselves until they mature to the next season of life.

The same is true in the spiritual realm. At the point of exasperation, we may want to shout at new believers, "Grow up!" But new believers who are beginning their Christian journey will not walk as mature believers. There are some things they have not learned yet. Their faith has not been tried.

But hearing these words will only frustrate new believers much as it frustrates little children to be told to "Grow up!"

Parents learn to focus on their children's behavior or the attitude that needs adjusting so that step by step and lesson by lesson the children grow into adulthood. Normal parents love their children in spite of their failures and inabilities; parents accept the fact that their children are works in progress.

Obviously, there are some childish adults in the world who would do well to heed the words, "Grow up!" But for young children as well as newly arrived Christians, patience and long-suffering are needed for the journey.

So, Mother and Father, let your children be children. This stage passes too quickly anyway; enjoy the process. And, brother or sister of God, let us be patient with our baby brothers and sisters. They will grow up—at the appointed time.

∞

Father, I'm your child. In you I find the strength to grow up. Develop in me a love that suffers long. I know how patient you have been with me, so I will be patient with others.

growth

Weekend Reflections

The gospel of the kingdom advances itself. Wherever it takes root, purity and righteousness will grow and spread. Your personal spiritual growth is nurtured by the power of God's Good News being planted in you. As the apostle Paul said, "All over the world this gospel is bearing fruit and growing, just as it has been doing among you since the day you heard it and understood God's grace in all its truth" (Col. 1:6).

1. If your growth depends on where you are planted, what is your responsibility?

   _____

   _____

   _____

   _____

2. To grow we must be willing to change. What positive changes have occurred in your life in the last six months?

   _____

   _____

   _____

   _____

3. The strong oak tree is a slow grower. Are you willing to be patient with others and with yourself as you grow in strength and maturity? What will be the evidence of this?

   _____

   _____

   _____

   _____

God's Growing Church

And I tell you that you are Peter, and on this rock I will build my church, and the gates of Hades will not overcome it.
—Matthew 16:18

Rest assured, Jesus is building his church at this very moment. Despite the inadequacy of mankind, our failures and weaknesses, God's plan is on schedule, because it is God's church and he is building it "on this rock."

And what is "this rock"? I believe it is the revelation knowledge of Jesus Christ—not just the knowledge that he is the Son of God but a continual revealing of Christ's nature, character, and power. This is not knowledge in the scientific sense but in the discerning sense. I don't claim to be a Greek scholar, even at the most elementary level, but I believe the Greek word used here does not describe mental knowledge but a knowledge that takes place at the heart level. If our knowledge—our revelation of Jesus—is not growing, then we can assume we are not growing, period. If a church's revelation of Jesus is not growing, then most likely the church is not growing in numbers or otherwise. As the wise man said, "By wisdom a house is built, and through understanding it is established; through knowledge its rooms are filled with rare and beautiful treasures" (Prov. 24:3–4).

∞

Lord Jesus, give me a hunger for knowledge of who you are—and not a mental knowledge but a heart knowledge. Oh, that I might have a fresh revelation of your brilliance, your majesty, your power. I wait now for a word from you.

The Great Pretenders

Another parable He put forth to them, saying: "The kingdom of heaven is like a man who sowed good seed in his field; but while men slept, his enemy came and sowed tares among the wheat and went his way."—Matthew 13:24–25 NKJV

It is unnerving to find out you have been duped. At one time or another, we've all said it: "How could I have been so blind?"

Perhaps you can relate to one of these situations:

- You meet someone who pretends to be your friend only to discover his or her motive was to sign you up for the latest pyramid sales scheme.
- You hire a promising young graduate for your business who leaves after six months with half your clientele.
- You listen to a desperate and needy person's story, hand him twenty dollars—and later learn you've been had by an impostor.

We've all been fooled at one time or another. Sadly, we're sometimes deceived by people even within the church; there are great pretenders there too. In his parable regarding the kingdom of heaven, Jesus made it clear that the wheat are his children and the tares are the pretenders the enemy has strategically placed in and among his people.

I have met those dear, disillusioned saints who wearily wander from church to church looking for one with no pretenders. If you're one of those wanderers, hang it up. There ain't one! (Excuse the slang.) As long as Satan is on the prowl and human beings exist on earth, there will be pretenders. But we can take comfort in knowing that God can tell the difference. He knows who's pretending and who isn't. His church is secure. As the apostle Paul wrote to young Timothy, "God's solid foundation stands firm, sealed with this inscription: 'The Lord knows those who are his'" (2 Tim. 2:19).

∞

Lord, I trust you to build your church as you said you would. I will not fret over those who pretend to know you but are only impostors. You will separate the tares from the wheat, and in the end "the righteous will shine like the sun" (Matt. 13:43).

God's church

One Big Family

You have not come to a mountain that can be touched.... But you
have come to Mount Zion, to the heavenly Jerusalem, the city of the
living God.—Hebrews 12:18, 22

Are you looking for a city where there are no fatherless children and
no childless moms and dads? There is one. But you can't just go visit it.
This is a members-only kind of place. But once you become a member,
you can live there forever. And when you're there, you are never alone.
You belong to a family that is innumerable.

The apostle Paul reminded the Hebrews that they were not heading
toward a place that could be touched or a place of darkness, gloom, and
storm. He was referring to Israel's fearful encounter with God at Mount
Sinai, but in this case he was not speaking of a literal mountain or city but
of a spiritual kingdom filled with "thousands upon thousands of angels in
joyful assembly,...the church of the firstborn, whose names are written in
heaven" (Heb. 12:22–23).

This is the heritage we have as believers. We don't have to divide it up
into shares; we get it all! In God's sight, every believer has the same rights.
It's as though we *all* get all the privileges of the firstborn. There are no sec-
onds or thirds, no oldest and youngest, no unwanted offspring—only
children who are loved and blessed, each one as if he or she were an only
child.

❧

God, I thank you that one of the names you have chosen for yourself is
Father. And you have called us your sons and daughters. Thank you for the
wonderful family that you have birthed me into.

THURSDAY

Is Church Boring to You?

He that believeth on me, as the scripture hath said, out of his belly shall flow rivers of living water.— John 7:38 KJV

From time to time, I have heard brothers and sisters in Christ say something like this: "I don't know what's happened. I just don't get anything out of church anymore. I mean, I love you guys and everything, but I'm just kind of bored with God and church." I can appreciate the frankness of someone who "tells it like it is." I think it's better to admit there's a problem than to go along pretending everything is fine. However, upon closer examination of those sentiments, I have to wonder whether this person's boredom is actually the work of the Spirit in his or her life? (I heard that gasp!) Maybe God has allowed church to get boring for a reason.

You see, God never meant for church services to be the end of it all. God's kingdom is so much bigger than going to church. It is a living, growing, moving entity. The gospel of Matthew says, "From the days of John the Baptist until now, the kingdom of heaven has been forcefully advancing, and forceful men lay hold of it" (11:12).

The church is where we get equipped to go out and do the works of Jesus. The kingdom principle is this: "Give, and it will be given to you" (Luke 6:38). Only as the life of God flows *out* of you will it flow *into* you. The Holy Spirit was not given just for our benefit and enjoyment. He did not come just so we would get together in church and feel goose bumps when the singing is especially beautiful and the preaching is especially effective. The Holy Spirit came to empower us to do the works of Jesus in the earth! We're the conduits through which the living water is to flow into the world. So if you don't feel anything coming in, examine what's going out!

∞

Lord, count me in. I want to be one the river flows through.

Unanswered Prayer

Neither pray I for these alone, but for them also which shall believe on me through their word; that they all may be one; as thou, Father, art in me, and I in thee, that they also may be one in us: that the world may believe that thou hast sent me.—John 17:20–21 KJV

Many times we hear nonbelievers say, "How can there be a God when there are so many different churches? They can't all be right!"

Quite possibly nothing has disillusioned the unsaved more than this one issue. Considering the multitude of denominations, it's easy to see how non-Christians are confused in their search for truth. The world will be more receptive to the Gospel when churches are more receptive to one another.

When he was here on earth, Jesus prayed we would all become one church, "that the world may believe that thou hast sent me." Because Christ could see through time, he saw the splintered, twentieth-century church, and he prayed that it could be mended so the hurting and needy could find a safe place to be restored to life again. Nearly two thousand years ago, in too many places, he prayed for us, but this prayer still goes unanswered.

Christians do not need to agree on every point to be the one body of Christ. We just need to sincerely share Christ's love with one another and unite in areas where we can make a difference. We must come together and stand on the one foundation that has been laid, the Cornerstone, Christ Jesus our Lord. There we will find a sure place, a solid Rock that is stable and secure. As we stand together there, we will be the answer to our Lord's prayer.

∞

Jesus, make us one, even as you and the Father are one. Help us to welcome those we have been unwilling to embrace. Bring your church together so that the world may believe and receive the gospel.

God's church

Weekend Reflections

All that is truly good in life is a gift from God. The beauty of creation and of people demonstrate the creativity and artistry of an amazing God. No one person completely reveals the character and beauty of God's personality except Christ. As Scripture tells us, "The Son is the radiance of God's glory and the *exact representation of his being,* sustaining all things by his powerful word" (Heb. 1:3, emphasis added). True Christians are all members of the same body; it takes all of us together to illustrate his body (see 1 Cor. 12:7). No one church or people can fully reveal Christ to the world.

1. Reflect on this week's readings and write down the examples of those who have demonstrated a certain aspect of God's character to you.

   _____

   _____

   _____

   _____

2. Observe the various traits in the different cultures that may be around you and describe how they may be useful in revealing Christ to the world.

   _____

   _____

   _____

   _____

3. If every Christian were exactly like you, what demonstration of God's nature to the world would be missing? (for example, boldness, serenity, cheerfulness, affection, etc.)

   _____

   _____

   _____

   _____

Beyond Knowledge

I pray that you…may have power…to grasp how wide and long and high and deep is the love of Christ, and to know this love that surpasses knowledge—that you may be filled to the measure of all the fullness of God.—Ephesians 3:17–19

As Christians, we know and believe that God loves us. We acknowledge his faithful, undying love for the Jewish nation as he delivered them from Egypt, and we comprehend the fact that his love for all the world was displayed on a hill called Golgotha.

But God's love goes way beyond knowledge. It cannot be confined in the work of a thousand commentaries and Bible study helps. It spills over the boundaries, disregarding man's intelligence and wisdom, splashing delightfully through the corridors of the hearts of those who pursue it. This love cannot be understood, but it can be experienced in the deep stillness of our souls as our spirits celebrate in deep communion with the Holy One.

Sometimes in prayer, with tears streaming down our faces and emotions so intense that words just don't come, sometimes we sense his love reaching out to us in ways that cannot be comprehended through mere intellect—for the intensity of his love is beyond knowing. And without any spoken communication, we commune with our Creator on a higher plane. We feel our spirits yearning within us crying "Abba, Abba!"and we know that we have connected with the love of God in a way that surpasses knowledge.

All who have found a new life in Christ know the love of God. In the position of repentance, we see our weakness and his perfection. But the love that goes beyond knowledge is gradually unfolded in us as we grow up and through him.

∽

Oh, the boundless love of God! Thank you, God, that life with you is never boring. There are always greater realms of your love yet to be revealed.

Forbearance

Be completely humble and gentle; be patient, bearing with one another in love.—Ephesians 4:2

Have you noticed how two people can look at the same thing and see something totally different or hear the same conversation and react in opposite ways? That's the idea that occurred to me when I talked with a lady who was upset because her pastor seemed to see only the good in people while ignoring the bad. Just once, she said, she wished he would agree with her that certain people really were a problem!

Many make the mistake of believing that God works with all of us in the same way, disregarding the fact that he considers each person's level of maturity in his dealings with us. God is looking for the best that each of us can do, not what we think that person should be doing. He is the all-knowing Father who understands that each of his children is unique. In contrast, Satan wants us to waste all of our time fighting with one another about our differences so we forget who our real enemy is.

In the natural realm, families that seem to work best and are the most nurturing are those that have high tolerance levels for individual differences. When difficulties arise among the family members, they acknowledge their differences but confidently say, "We're a family; we can work it out."

God's church should be like that family—a place where all his different children, the godly and obedient as well as the wounded and oppressed—can come and find peace. But instead of being a haven of rest, sometimes the church is more like the den of strife; peace is just a pause between arguments, "that glorious brief moment when everyone stops to reload," as John MacArthur described it.

God's true love is forbearing, "ready to believe the best of every person" (1 Cor. 13:7 AMPLIFIED). As Paul wrote to the Ephesians, God is our peace, the One who tore down the "dividing wall of hostility" (Eph. 2:14). Let's leave that wall down and follow our Father's example.

∞

Jesus, you are the one who destroyed the walls of division between your people. What weapons have I taken up to use against my brothers and sisters? Reveal them to me, and I will destroy them. Give us the grace to forbear with each other as we grow up into you.

He's Got the Whole World in His Hand

The earth is the Lord's, and everything in it. The world and all its people belong to him.—Psalm 24:1 NLT

Travel virtually anywhere, and you will find tragedy.

In certain countries of Africa, the AIDS epidemic is so great that the government can't build enough hospitals for the victims to die in. In China, the government's idea of family planning is forced abortion. There are countries where ten-year-olds become prostitutes to support their family. In other nations parents willingly give their children to temple priests so the family can receive absolution for crimes committed.

Such atrocities shock us and break our hearts. We weep. We send money. We go to the ends of the earth to try and help, and yet the tragedies continue. Still, our Father has called us, commanded us, to heal the sick, to bear another's burden, to give to the poor—and we must obey. We must do what we can.

When we feel that our efforts are insignificant, wondering whether one person can really make a difference, we must believe the answer is an earnest *yes*. God doesn't expect us to heal the world all by ourselves, but he reminds us that even a "cup of water" in Christ's name will not go unseen by heaven's eyes (see Mark 9:41).

God is orchestrating a symphony of love. While one Christian ministers to a dying AIDS patient, one translates the Scripture for a lost tribe of primitive people. While one holds a baby born addicted to drugs, another gives a cup of cool water to a thirsty child. We do what we can while recognizing there is only one Lord of the harvest, and it's not one of us. God is the one who gives the increase.

❦

Father, you are the giver of life. You see the sparrow that falls and know the number of hairs on our heads. You know each helpless child and hurting heart by name. Not one of them hurts without your knowledge.

Jesus Is Loving You!

Now you are the body of Christ, and each one of you is a part of it.
—1 Corinthians 12:27

Those of us who are fortunate enough to know Wayne Francis have endearingly nicknamed him Saint Francis. We call him that because we've found that it's nearly impossible for anyone to be around Wayne very long before he finds a way to minister to that person. Whether in a practical or a spiritual way, he inevitably reveals his heart for others—buying a meal, offering up a prayer, leading someone to Christ, or simply speaking God's word in a fresh way.

Most of us admire folks like Wayne and want to be around them. They have learned to manifest the nature of Christ and have become conduits of God's living water to the world. When we are with them, they energize and inspire us. We feel like better people when we have been with them.

Everyone wants to feel loved and cared for. We want to be assured that God knows our names and where we live. While we are looking for some miraculous sign—an angel, a flash of light, or a voice in the night—God's love and concern for us are quite evident in the common human beings he sends to minister to us. They are the ones who live out his life-giving words in their kindness to others.

The warmth and love we sense from the pure in heart is *Christ's* warmth and love. The goodness that flows from these brothers and sisters is none other than the goodness of *Christ himself.* It flows from his fountain through them as a blessing to us. So if we are better people for having known a Saint Francis, let us remember that it really isn't him or her. It is Jesus himself, loving us through a member of his body.

∞

Dear God, thank you for those you have sent to speak your word into my life. I know, Lord, that it is really you shining through them, so I thank you for your love that I see in them.

A Passionate God

When God created man, he made him in the likeness of God.
—Genesis 5:1

He loves. He hates. He laughs. He cries. He embraces. He kisses. He shouts. He whispers. He sings. He grieves. (See John 3:16; Prov. 6:16; Ps. 2:4; John 11:35; Luke 15:20; Jer. 25:30; 1 Kings 19:12; Zeph. 3:17; 1 Chron. 21:15.)

Some reject such a passionate God. They prefer a God who is detached, removed, and tucked away in a cathedral where we can go visit him. Don't give them a God who is active, intimate, and passionate. After all, how could God be truly God and have those kinds of passions?

Where do you think we got the capacity to love, hate, weep, and rejoice if not from our Father? We were created in the *likeness* of God (see Gen. 5:1). It was God himself who placed our complex souls in us. And if we have the capacity for such passions, we can only attempt to conceive a God whose passions are infinitely beyond our own. The goodness of our emotions are but shadows of the all-consuming passions of the infinite heart of God.

Just imagine the heaviest grief you have known. Jesus sorrowed more. Remember your highest joys? His joy is fuller still. Think of the times you were angered because of the lack of justice for the innocent. God was angered more. Imagine the greatest love you have seen demonstrated, then know that God's love is deeper, higher, longer, and wider than that— and purer.

∞

Lord Jesus, give me a greater understanding of who you are. Help me know that you have experienced the depths of grief and have loved us through the Cross. Help me grasp the fact that you don't just extend love to us, that you are love.

God is love

Weekend Reflections

God's love is the forbearing kind, "ready to believe the best of every person" (1 Cor. 13:7 AMPLIFIED). Instead of seeing us in our weakness, God's love sees our needs.

1. We are commanded to love as we have been loved (see John 13:34). Considering the qualities of Christ's love for us, how should we love others?

_____

_____

_____

_____

_____

_____

2. Jesus loves us through others. Thinking back over this week, how has Christ loved you through someone else.

_____

_____

_____

_____

3. The Bible tells us God's love cannot be confined to knowledge (see Eph. 3:19). How, then, do we comprehend this love?

_____

_____

_____

_____

Choose Joy!

Be joyful at your Feast—you, your sons and daughters, your men-servants and maidservants, and the Levites, the aliens, the fatherless and the widows who live in your towns.—Deuteronomy 16:14

Being joyful is more of a decision than a feeling. We "decide" to be joyful at different levels of consciousness. For the happy-go-lucky types, joyfulness is often a choice made at a subconscious plane. Nevertheless, I believe it is choice, an assent of the will. For most of us, however, the decision to be joyful sometimes takes a little more effort. Christmas may be one of those times.

Christmas is a time for celebration, good cheer, and joy. But just because it's the "time" for those feelings doesn't mean we automatically feel them. Tragedy or disappointment may have knocked the wind out of you, leaving you feeling anything but joyful. But there is still reason to rejoice. If you are struggling with pain or sorrow as the holiday approaches, I urge you to awaken your heart and hear the "good tidings of great joy" (Luke 2:10 KJV).

The news the angels brought to the shepherds was not just to herald Christ's birth for the world but to say, "Today…a Savior has been born to you" (v. 11). Your reason to rejoice on Christmas Day is that Christ was born for you as much as for anyone else in the world. And one of the reasons Emmanuel came to be with us is to bring you comfort and joy. He said, "These things I have spoken unto you, that in me ye might have peace. In the world ye shall have tribulation: but be of good cheer; I have overcome the world" (John 16:33 KJV).

Lay aside the hurt that overshadows your joy. Celebrate the birth of the One who came to take your burdens upon himself. Make a conscious decision to let his peace and joy fill your heart.

❧

Lord Jesus, thank you for the day that stands as a reminder to us of how you humbled yourself and became a babe in a manger. The joy I have is more than a feeling of Christmas spirit. It is birthed from the realization that you were born for even me.

A Heart Full of Treasures

But Mary treasured up all these things and pondered them in her heart.—Luke 2:19

Some things are meant to be treasured in our hearts. They seem to lose some of their loveliness when they are flaunted publicly.

Have you ever been around a married couple when they start discussing their personal business in front of you? Feels awkward, doesn't it? The Spirit sometimes reveals to me things that are just too personal to become common knowledge. They are part of my private conversations with God, topics reserved for personal discussions with my Creator.

Perhaps God shares some things with you, too, that are not meant to be shared with the whole world or even with your circle of friends and family members. God may want you to show some restraint and keep those things between you and him. That was true for the apostle Paul. In 2 Corinthians 12:4 he said he heard things in heavenly places that "man is not permitted to tell."

When they are treasured and spoken at the right time, words have a beauty they would not have if they were pretentiously trumpeted about. They become like the king's crown jewels, displayed only for the right occasion, or "like apples of gold in settings of silver" (Prov. 25:11 NKJV).

∞

Lord Jesus, thank you for the words of life you have spoken to my spirit. Certainly there have been times when I have said things I should not have said and shared things openly that were meant to treasured. Please forgive me and grant me the discernment to know what things I should ponder in my heart and what things should be shared with others.

When God Rejoiced

*The Lord your God is with you, he is mighty to save. He will take
great delight in you, he will quiet you with his love, he will rejoice
over you with singing.*—Zephaniah 3:17

To *rejoice* means "to experience joy and gladness to a high degree."
Children know how to rejoice. Just visit a classroom on the day before
Christmas vacation.

Adults, on the other hand, rarely rejoice. Think about it. When was
the last time you rejoiced? What was the occasion?

I grew up in a culture that generally considered rejoicing rather
uncouth. Especially if it were done openly—and even more so if the
"rejoicer" was a man. A man who exuberantly rejoiced in public was considered immature and silly. Such a scene was noted and remarked upon.
It became a matter of conversation: "Did you see how excited Bill got
when his son scored the winning touchdown? He made quite a spectacle
of himself." By his unrestrained behavior, Bill showed a side of himself
others didn't normally get to see.

The most interesting thing to me is seeing what God has chosen to
rejoice about. Certainly, these were not the same things you and I would
rejoice about today. For example, in Luke 10:21, Jesus rejoiced because
the Father chose to reveal the working of the kingdom to "little children"
and let it be hidden from the wise. This is the same God who splashed the
sky with stars, rolled out the universe, and stooped to breathe into Adam's
nostrils the breath of life—and then simply said that it was "good."
Instead, he gets excited about simple people becoming partakers of his
heritage, about one sinner repenting, about one prodigal son finding his
way home, about one sheep returning to the flock.

Think about these things that God rejoiced over. Then think about
the last time you rejoiced enough to cause someone to notice.

❦

Father, every day there is reason to rejoice. Let me celebrate the things you
celebrate and delight in what you love.

What's in a Name?

Therefore God exalted him to the highest place and gave him the name that is above every name.—Philippians 2:9

Our names are the titles we answer to, the words that identify us. Parents spend hours choosing names for their babies before they're born because a name is closely linked to their child's character. That's why you don't find many Judases or Jezebels in baby name books.

The Bible teaches us that God began his covenant with man by naming himself. It says God's name was *revealed* first, not that it was given to him by some man. Those names came later, when great men walked with God and began to know him. As he *revealed* himself to them, they gave him other names. For example, when God provided a ram for Abraham, he called God *Jehovah-Jireh,* meaning "God, my provider." And as God was revealed, he was also named *Jehovah-Roi,* meaning "God, my shepherd," and *Jehovah-Shalom,* meaning "God, my peace."

The prophets saw glimpses of the future when God said he would reveal himself by a mightier name that they could not know. It was not given to them to know because God had not yet *revealed* it. But today we have the privilege of knowing that name Jesus.

Do you know why there is such power in Jesus' name? Because God gave that name to him: "Therefore God exalted him to the highest place and *gave him* the name that is above every name, that at the name of Jesus every knee should bow" (Phil. 2:9–10, emphasis added).

God has been revealed as our Jesus, which means he is our Savior. But unless you have received the revelation of him into your own life, Jesus is just a name.

God, I praise you for the way you have revealed yourself to us through the name of your Son. I willingly bow my knee today and worship his name, for you have always been God, but now you are my Savior. You are my Jesus.

God with Me

Behold, a virgin shall be with child, and shall bring forth a son, and
they shall call his name Emmanuel, which being interpreted is,
God with us.—Matthew 1:23 KJV

For generations, men and women longed for God, but very few ever saw him. The prophet Isaiah spoke the heart of many when he cried, "O that you would tear open the heavens and come down, so that the mountains would quake at your presence" (64:1 NRSV). This man, Isaiah, was one of the select few who saw him. Along with other men of renown like Moses, Abraham, and Jacob, Isaiah would see God and converse with God in a real way on this clay sphere we call home.

I wonder what it was like to see God in that way, this God they had prayed and sacrificed to, the God they had heard about and feared, the One behind the awesome displays of power they had witnessed. Finally, he stood before them and talked with them.

Only a few such events were recorded for thousands of years. Then God surprised all of humanity and appeared, not to only a few, but to the world—as a baby! He would grow up to be a man who would walk, talk, and eat as all people do. His body of flesh would be subject to the same frailties as ours. He would get drowsy, even exhausted, feel the sting of pain, and the aching of grief. He would be God…with us and like us.

And now, the wonder of that awesome truth becomes even more astonishing: He is not only God with *us* but God with *me*. He is not just a God who visits me when I pray or sees me when I go to church. He is *with* me always: when I am in the kitchen, on the sofa, at the office, in the car, at the store, in a crowd—everywhere, every moment! And though I sometimes feel alone, I am *never* really alone, because God—*my* God and yours too—is with me.

❧

Lord Jesus, I thank you for being unwilling to know us only from a distance. You are not only God of this world, but you are God with us. And even better, now you are God with me. I am never alone. Whatever I face, I face with you by my side. When I laugh, you are there. When I cry, you are there. You are my Emmanuel.

celebrate Christ

Weekend Reflections

One of the incredible truths about Christmas is that God became a baby. Not a child. Not a man. But a helpless, hungry, crying infant. God came into our world, not in a flaming chariot, but through the womb of a young virgin named Mary. Such a truth gives us reason to call this "the season of wonder" and to celebrate the angels' announcement: "Today…a Savior has been born to you" (Luke 2:11). Take a moment to "wonder" about other *wonderful* components of the Christmas story.

1. Why didn't God prepare a room for Mary and Joseph at the inn? Why was Jesus born in a stable?

_____

_____

_____

_____

2. Why did the angels sing in the countryside instead of the Bethlehem town square?

_____

_____

_____

_____

3. Mary believed what the angel said. Could *you* have believed such an incredible promise? Explain your answer.

_____

_____

_____

_____

change

We Shall Be Like Him

*But we all, with open face beholding as in a glass the glory of the
Lord, are changed into the same image from glory to glory, even as by
the Spirit of the Lord.*—2 Corinthians 3:18 KJV

The more we see Jesus, the more we become like him. We reflect what
we come in contact with.

There is an unmistakable glow on the face of one who has received
the Holy Spirit. It happens because the natural has met the supernatural.
The temporal has encountered the eternal.

When we experience God this way, when we see his glory, we are
changed. Something happens to us in the spiritual realm. Oh, we may
look the same on the outside. Our noses will still be in the same place,
and our ears will be the same size, but something spiritual definitely happens. We become more like him. We are changed into the same image—
his image—"from glory to glory." And we go from his presence reflecting
what we have seen. This is the continual working of the Holy Spirit: to
change us until we look, think, and act like Jesus.

The longer we know him, the more we should look like him, not so
much because of what we are doing, but because of what the Spirit is
doing in us. And this change goes on until that time when we no longer
look through a dark glass but see him face to face. In that moment, whatever remains of us that is not like him will instantly be changed! The
Bible says, "What we will be has not yet been made known. But we know
that when he appears, we shall be like him, for we shall see him as he is"
(1 John 3:2).

∞

Dear God, I want to be more like you. May I hunger more for your presence
so that I will see your glory and be changed into your image, reflecting your
glory, your character, your power in the earth.

TUESDAY

What about Real Change?

Instead, we will hold to the truth in love, becoming more and more in
every way like Christ, who is the head of his body, the church.
—Ephesians 4:15 NLT

For most of us, change doesn't come easily. As Christians we want to change—to become ever more Christlike. But some days we wonder if we're making any progress, because, when we're honest with ourselves, we just don't *feel* like we're changing.

If you find yourself in this predicament, let me offer you some encouragement. First, the fact that you desire change is something to be thankful for. It is the holiness and purity of God's Spirit within you that isolates and rejects whatever is ungodly in you and calls you to change. This realization should bring about true humility and also help you understand that your desire to change is not self-generated; the urge itself is your indication that the Spirit is already working for change in you!

Jesus said, "I tell you the truth, unless you *change* and become like little children, you will never enter the kingdom of heaven" (Matt. 18:3, emphasis added). Consider what a great application this has for us as we impatiently wait to change into more Christlike people. As a child grows, he may feel as if he is not growing at all. The normal response from the parent at that point is, "Just keep eating right and taking your vitamins and you'll see: You *will* grow. You just can't see it from one day to the next." Changes in the spiritual realm work the same way. We look to our heavenly Father and say, "Will I ever be like you someday? I don't feel like I'm changing at all!"

And his patient words come back to us: "Do what you know to do. Keep my words in your heart; spend time with me, and you'll see. Growth will come."

∞

Father, I know you are the only real source of change. Please strengthen my desire to become more like you. Help me to walk in your ways, living the spiritual disciplines, so that I will be in position for your Holy Spirit to transform me into your likeness.

Leave Change Up to God

*Have I not chosen you, the Twelve? Yet one of you is
a devil!*—John 6:70

Changing other people is a futile, wearisome job. That is why, if we're
smart, we'll leave the people-changing up to God. It's funny, really, to
think we can actually change others when we don't even have the power
to change ourselves!

We need to remember this fact lest we start believing such lies as, *If
only I could be more of an example, my spouse would be a better Christian.*
Jesus was the best example there ever was, yet in the end one of the Twelve
betrayed him and the rest scattered in fear. Jesus understood that his disciples exerted their own will power. He did not take it as defeat when they
scattered. Surely, it did hurt. Surely, he felt the pangs of loneliness and
abandonment. But his confidence was in the power of God, the One who
had brought them to him in the first place and who, he knew, would keep
them. He prayed in the garden, "Holy Father, keep through Your name
those whom You have given Me, that they may be one as We are" (John
17:11 NKJV).

This is a message of peace to the parent who is laden with guilt
because a wayward son or daughter continues in a dangerous, frivolous
lifestyle despite the parent's doing everything possible to keep that child
walking safely in God's path. And it's a message to lift the burden of the
weary pastor who is discouraged by the level of spiritual maturity in his
congregation. It's reassurance to the wife who yearns for her husband to
walk in the godly role he was created for. To all of you, this message says,
"Place your hope in God, not in yourself. Be free from the guilt, the
shame, the despair!"

We are to be examples, yes, of praying, believing, and hoping for
change in those we love. But as we pray and believe, let us fix our eyes on
the Changer of human beings' hearts. We follow Jesus' example of loving,
serving, and praying for those we hold dear. Then we place our dear ones
in the arms of the One who gave them to us in the first place.

God, I repent of trying to change people. I give them up to you, the Changer
of men. Jesus, I pray according to your Word, "keep them through your
name."

change

Growth Means Change

*The Spirit of the Lord will come upon you in power, and you will
prophesy with them; and you will be changed into
a different person.*—1 Samuel 10:6

After the prophet Samuel anointed Saul to be the new king over Israel, Samuel gave him specific instructions. He told Saul to go up to the mountain where "the Spirit of the Lord will come upon you in power, and you will prophesy with them; and you will be changed into a different person" (1 Sam. 10:6).

God could not use Saul the way he was, but Saul's obedience would bring about a radical change that would equip him for the coming challenges as a king. Within just a few days, the safety of his kingdom would be threatened, and the old Saul would not know what to do.

Every new level of spiritual growth requires us to change. If we're not willing to change, we can't grow. That's why I spell growth c-h-a-n-g-e!

Children cannot become adults without going through the awkward changes that occur in adolescence. No one can bypass this stage. It is a requirement. It may be uncomfortable, difficult to understand, and downright humbling, but before you enjoy the rights of adulthood, you have to learn the lessons of childhood.

What level of spiritual maturity are you crying out for? What new "rights" of fellowship with God do you desire? Perhaps it is a higher level of ministry. Perhaps it is closer intimacy with God. When you want to grow into a higher level of understanding as a Christian, you must be willing to change.

Now, change can be difficult. In fact, it can be downright impossible sometimes! So the relieving hope for Christians is that it is God who initiates and affects change in our lives. We don't have to do it on our own. Real change comes as we let the Holy Spirit do the changing. "The Spirit of the Lord will come upon you...and you will be changed."

∞

Lord, show me where I have resisted change. I want to say yes to your Spirit, knowing that my change will come not by my own might or power but by your Spirit.

A Time to Throw Away

*A time to search and a time to lose. A time to keep and a time
to throw away.*—Ecclesiastes 3:6 NLT

Are you one of those people who saves everything—just in case you might need it someday? Does the conversation on spring-cleaning day at your house sound something like this: "No! You can't throw that away. You never know when we might need it."

Some of us need to have spring cleaning of our minds. What outdated beliefs and remnants of guilt are lying around cluttering up your thoughts? What problems have you been avoiding dealing with? What dilemma have you been shelving, just hoping it will disappear? Deal with it! There is a time to throw things away, and for many of us, we're overdue!

Zig Ziglar has said that one way to have a better, more productive day is to make the thing you dread most a priority. That phone call you don't want to make—do it first. That assignment you can't bear to face—start it now. Rather than allowing something unpleasant to consume your energy all day long, get it over and done with. Clean your mental house!

For inspiration, read the story of young King Josiah, who became king at the ripe old age of eight! Josiah spent most of his years as king throwing away things. He cleansed the land of idols, false gods, and false images, and he led his nation into a time of blessing and consecration (see 2 Kings 22:1—23:29). He discovered the power of the "time to throw away."

❧

Lord, you have shown us the importance of discarding things that need to be discarded. You have thrown away all of our sins into the depths of the sea (see Mic. 7:19). You have set a time to throw away. I will follow your example.

change

Weekend Reflections

The end of the year is a good time to examine where we are in our Christian walk as well as where we want to be. Change is a big part of achieving our goals—not change for the sake of change, but changes that will stretch us in some way. As John Maxwell wrote in his book *Living at the Next Level,* "If you keep doing what you've always done, you'll always get what you've always gotten."

1. What one change could you make right now in your journey toward Christian maturity that would be a major step toward reaching your goal?

   _____

   _____

   _____

   _____

   _____

2. Take a look inside your mental closet. What do you need to throw away?

   _____

   _____

   _____

   _____

   _____

3. There are some things you cannot change without God's intervention. What changes can you make that will move you into a position where God can change what you cannot change?

   _____

   _____

   _____

   _____